The armed Prussian state yacht *Fridericus Rex*, copperplate engraving by J. G. Wolfgang about 1710.

The Ships of
the German Fleets
1848-1945

Hans Jürgen Hansen

Naval Institute Press

Technical adviser: Fregattenkapitän Heinz von Bassi,
Former Principal of the Historical Collection at the
Marineschule, Flensburg-Mürwik

© Urbes Verlag Hans Jürgen Hansen
Published and distributed by the Naval Institute Press, Annapolis, Maryland 21402
Library of Congress Catalog Card No. 87-63367
ISBN 0-87021-654-6
This edition is authorized for sale in the English language
Made and printed in the Federal Republic of Germany by
Druckhaus Neue Stalling GmbH & Co KG, D-2900 Oldenburg

Contents

Foreword

This book aims to give a clear picture of the ships of the German national fleets which were responsible for a century of German naval prestige, beginning with the foundation of the navy of the democratic Reich in 1848 and ending at the close of the war in 1945. It also describes Germany's part in a worldwide phenomenon which, though recent, is hard to appreciate fully today. For only very few examples survive from this exceedingly interesting period in the development of shipbuilding; and only a few of the famous older warships have been preserved and put on display: Gustavus Adolphus's *Vasa* of 1632 is in Stockholm and Nelson's *Victory* of 1806 in Portsmouth. But we shall never see again any of the huge warships built in this century, as the last remaining example, the former German *Goeben,* was broken up in Turkey, in 1979.

The preparation of this book entailed the unearthing and sifting of a great deal of unpublished and half-forgotten picture material in archives, museums and collections. I became convinced that here was a unique opportunity to try to convey, by means of illustrations, an impression of this relatively recent but most important chapter in German naval history. The work is therefore copiously illustrated, with reproductions of paintings, watercolours, drawings, engravings, lithographs and many contemporary photographs. (A technical point should be mentioned here: a number of the older lantern slides, for which the original plates are no longer available, show signs of retouching of the negative. This was done at the time and cannot be removed without damaging the value of the slides as documents or reducing the quality of reproduction.)

My treatment of the material is based on the following premise: in 1848 the first-ever regular fleet belonging to the whole German-speaking realm was formed. However, whilst Austrian and Prussian warships fought with Germany as late as 1864, against Denmark, it was only after the setting-up of the North German Federation in 1867 that a purely German fleet developed, in the same way as did the newly-established state itself. Thus I have not dealt with ships launched in Austria after 1866.

The text is intended to complement the illustrations. It includes important technical details and histories of the vessels illustrated, and gives a brief outline of general developments. Detailed figures are given, however, only where they seem essential for the appreciation of the size, speed and fighting strength of the ships. Thus the overall length (without jib-boom, etc.) in metres (m) is chiefly given, as also is the tonnage—that is (unless otherwise stated) the structural weight (displacement at the waterline) in metric tons (t), and in some cases also the standard displacement in English tons (ts); or for older ships before 1860, the volume in gross registered tons (GRT). Information is given, where it may be helpful, about crew strengths, armament and speed. Throughout, the highest speed attained is given in knots (nautical miles per hour)—this usually exceeded the design speed.

This book would have been impossible without advice, encouragement and willing help, for which I am indebted (in addition to those lenders of pictures named elsewhere) to Dr. Jobst in Bremen and Dr. Schlepps in Kiel, also to Mr. Edward H. H. Archibald in Greenwich, Dr. Friedrich Car-

stens in Brake, Dr. Klaus Grimm in Hamburg, Franz Hahn in Flensburg, Helmut Kleffel in Kiel, Arnold Kludas in Hamburg, Alexander von Petöfi in Bremen-Vegesack, Dr. Burchhard Scheper and Gert Schlechtriem in Bremerhaven and Lieutenant-Commander Heinz Stoelzel in Cuxhaven—but above all to Commander Heinz von Bassi, Keeper of the Historical Collection at Mürwik Naval College, who painstakingly checked the manuscript and illustrations.

Having completed the work, I find it hard, as a former naval man, to resist making certain personal observations about the ideals of splendour, glory and heroism in the German fleets. The story of the flag, which I have encountered again and again, is an example of these. It tells of the sinking of the gunboat *Iltis* in July 1896 off the coast of China. Apparently the crew gave three cheers for the Kaiser and then struck up the so-called "Flag Song" before the ship went down:
"Loyal and devoted ever,
True until we're dead,
We shall cease to serve it never,
Flag of black-white-red!"

No one who like the author has himself witnessed the loss of ships and of dozens of naval colleagues; no one who was also often required to sing of his faith in the all-important flag will easily conquer his aversion for phrases of this kind. These sentiments were embodied in the painting *The Last Man,* which was reproduced many thousands of times during the First World War. Standing without support on the keel of a capsized cruiser in the Atlantic, off the Falkland Islands, the man flourishes the battle flag. Further back in time there is another saying, in Latin, which arouses scepticism: *Navigare necesse est—vivere non est necesse.* I firmly maintain that sea travel, while wholly necessary, would be useless if we believed life to be without purpose.

For most of the navy men who lost their lives while serving on German warships the end was quite unheroic. If they were not first trapped in a sinking ship, they would be reduced to desperate blowing on the emergency whistles which were attached to their life-jackets, in the hope that someone would hear. When they no longer had breath to blow, there would be only hopelessness, slow freezing and at length unconsciousness. If the water was cold it would all be over within half an hour. And then would come the gulls, the vultures of the ocean.

That was the nature of a hero's death at sea.

Whilst I have made my personal feelings plain on this score, I should stress that I consider it inadmissible and even a little un-dignified to make light of the momentous historical reality and great political significance of the German fleet, or of the equally real national power and naval prestige which it embodied. Certainly the fleet had, at least under Wilhelm II and Tirpitz, something monstrous about it, but it was nonetheless the object of enormous popular support.

At a time when worldwide air travel and mass tourism were unknown, the navy offered young men from less well-to-do homes what was often their only chance to travel the world. "Join the Navy and see the world": this successful recruiting slogan of the American Navy was also the catchphrase for the young men from Saxony and Bavaria who went to serve in the German fleet. But joining the Navy did not mean one instantly saw the world. No-one who merely wanted to do his military service in the Navy would be stationed on a warship. Such positions were offered to professional seamen only. But longer-serving volunteers applied in droves, and in spite of the rigours which sailors had to withstand during military and other voyages, there was still enough romance of the La Paloma kind, and plenty of globetrotting ambitions were still fulfilled—as long as there was no war.

Yet the fact remains that this fleet, as a politico-military institution and repository of power for a German-speaking or expanded German national state, ran aground just as that state did itself. That, however, is no reason to forget it—it was too significant, too impressive and had (I use the word advisedly) too much historical greatness to be easily forgotten. It also had its share of tragedy, and the memory of the thousands of crew members who fell in vain in two World Wars should be cherished.

I trust that this book will at least serve as a memorial to these men, and so I dedicate it to those comrades of mine who remained at sea—those who were not, like me, lucky enough to come back home safely.

Amrum Island   Hans Jürgen Hansen

January 1988

German Warships before 1848

In contrast with all other leading European coastal states, the old Roman state of Germany never possessed its own naval force. This is not to say that there were no warships in the harbours of the state which broke up in 1805, nor that none had until then been built in German shipyards. But a state organization was lacking, the central authority of a national Admiralty, such as existed in England, France, Sweden, Denmark, Spain, Portugal and the Netherlands, and such as the naval powers of Venice, Genoa and Naples also possessed, to their considerable advantage.

Yet, like the history of the German nation, so too its maritime history begins with Charlemagne: he found it essential to fit out warships to secure his coasts against the Frisians and Normans at the mouths of the Rhine, and against the Moors in the Mediterranean.

In the 11th and 12th centuries ships from the Lower Rhine, from Frisia and from the Weser took part in the Crusades; and later the Hanseatic towns had at their disposal armed convoy ships for the defence of their trade routes.

Wallenstein, as "General of the Oceanic and Baltic Seas", tried in 1628 to assemble a fleet in Wismar, but failed in the face of a successful Swedish blockade of the north German harbour which he had occupied.

Brandenburg and Austria subsequently made several starts at creating fleets. Elector Friedrich Wilhelm chartered a few frigates and smaller vessels in Holland for the encounters with Sweden, and was able to capture from the enemy the frigate *Mohrian*, which together with the frigate *Churprinz* in 1683 founded the colony of Grossfriedrichsburg on the African coast of Guinea.

Churprinz and *Mohrian,* for which plans no longer exist, are depicted with historical accuracy as they fall upon the Guinea coast on 1st January 1683 in this painting by Alexander Kircher. They represent typical Dutch warships of the time.

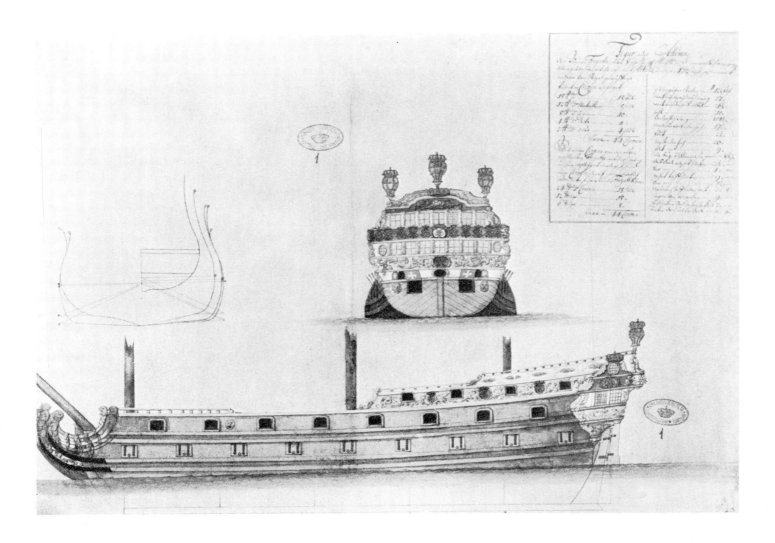

At the time there was for a while a Brandenburg Admiralty with a naval station for the North Sea at Emden and one for the Baltic at Pillau. Similarly, Austria maintained an arsenal in Trieste at the beginning of the 18th century, as well as a fleet of its own ships-of-the-line and frigates. But these activities were of little significance. What is more, the Brandenburg ships were mostly built in the Netherlands, while the Austrian ones were built in Italian ports, and these, indeed, had wholly Italian crews. In Germany itself, the Hanseatic towns of Hamburg, Bremen, Lübeck and Danzig were almost alone in having efficient shipyards capable of building larger sea-going vessels. In fact, since all ocean-going trading ships up to the beginning of the 19th century had

to be heavily armed against pirates, these were not fundamentally different from the warships of the same period. A Hamburg vessel on the West Indies route was only slightly less well armed than, for example, a Dutch ship of the line—only the need for greater cargo space reduced the armaments. In the 18th century, in all the larger German harbours, were to be found the so-called trading frigates, in which the one and only gun deck was over the hold.

The ruling princes of the German coastal territories and the officials of the Hanseatic towns at that time maintained so-called state yachts, fast sailing show vessels, along the lines of Dutch and English models. These generally had free-standing cannon on either side of the deck. Even the Elector

of the Palatinate, who lived in Mannheim, owned one of these state yachts, built in Amsterdam, and used it on the Rhine.

A copper engraving, after a painting by the court painter Madersteg, of the particularly luxurious state yacht *Fridericus Rex,* has been preserved. Frederick I of Prussia had her built in Belgium and brought over the North and Baltic Seas and up the Oder to the lakes of Brandenburg. She was described as a *Liburnica,* the old name for fast vessels of the galley type, and was sumptuously decorated with carvings and paintings, the figurehead showing the king himself on horseback. The ship was about 26 m long, more than 7 m beam and fitted out with 22 heavy bronze cannon (see illustration opposite title page).

A copper engraving, dating from 1755, of a somewhat smaller and more modest Hanseatic yacht belonging to the Hamburg Admiralty, also exists. The yacht had eight guns—exact dimensions are not known (picture above).

Neither plans nor specifications remain of pre-1800 ships flying Brandenburg or Austrian flags. The oldest plan still extant of a warship built in a German shipyard, at Neumühlen on the Elbe, which now belongs to Hamburg but which then was administered as part of Holstein from Copenhagen, is that of the Elbe frigate *Stormarn* which sailed under the Danish flag. It was drawn in 1703—with stern and side views of the hull, diagrams of the ribs and detailed data on dimensions (picture above

left), and is now in the Orlogsmuseet in Copenhagen.

After the Congress of Vienna and the founding of the German Federation, Austria and Prussia alone retained war vessels—and then only in modest numbers. The Austrian fleet, manned exclusively with Italian crews and stationed in Venice, consisted in 1826 of the frigates *Bellona* and *Ebe*, the corvette *Carolina*, the brigs *Veloce, Orion, Veneto, Montecuccoli, Ussaro, San Maro* and *Emo*, the schooners *Sofia, Fenize, Aretusa, Arianne, Vigilante, Enrichetta* and *Elisabetta*, the pinnaces *Najade* and *Vestale*, the troopships *Bravo* and *Justo*, and the hospital ship *Spaviero*, altogether (except for the two frigates) 22 relatively small wooden sailing vessels.

After the cession of Stralsund by the Swedes, Prussia took over six Swedish gun sloops, together with their two Swedish commanding officers Longé and Murck, who remained until 1848 the only naval officers in the Prussian fleet. In 1816 an armed schooner was launched by the J. A. Meyer shipyard in Stralsund and was given the same name as the town. This *Stralsund* was the first new warship specifically constructed for Prussia. The gunboats appropriated from Sweden proved to be unusable and were sold in 1817/19—the same thing happened to the schooner *Stralsund* in 1829. In 1827 Longé became head and Murck pay officer of the Prussian "Marine-Etablissement" set up on the island of Dänholm opposite Stralsund.

Plans for founding a fleet were tentatively considered in Prussia, but came to nothing. In April 1841 King Frederick William IV directed that an ocean-going corvette be built as a training ship for the further instruction of pupils from the College of Navigation which had in the meantime been founded in Danzig. On the 24th June 1843, she was launched by the Carmesin shipyard in Grabow near Stettin, bearing the name *Amazone*. The ships' builders and, in large part, their tools and equipment as well, came from outside Germany, whilst the rigging was carried out by Danish non-commissioned officers. She was carvel-built out of oak, was about 34 m long and 9 m beam and, with full rigging, which meant a sail area of 876 sqm, could do 11 knots. She was equipped with 12 Swedish 18-pounder cannon; the crew numbered 6 officers and 139 men. In 1844 she made her first foreign voyage into the Black Sea; in 1845 she sailed via Madeira to Genoa; in 1847 she visited New York; and in 1852/53 South America. In November 1861, in the southern part of the North Sea, she was lost in a violent storm with her crew and the cadets who were also on board—107 men. She is remembered as the "Grandmother of the German Fleet".

In the above painting by L. Arenhold, in the Mürwik Naval College, she is shown firing a salute to port.

The flush-decked corvette *Mercur,* shown in the painting by L. Arenhold reproduced above, was launched by J. Klawitter in Danzig in 1847 as an East Indiaman of the Prussian Sea-Trading Company. In March 1850 she was purchased by the Prussian Fleet. She too was a wooden carvel-built ship and, fully rigged, had a sail area of 805 sqm. About 43 m long and 8 m beam, the *Mercur* weighed 650 GRT, could sail at 9 knots and was equipped with six 26-pounder carronades. She served also as a training ship for the instruction of cadets and in November set forth on her first foreign voyage to Rio de Janeiro via Tenerife. In 1861 she was broken up in Danzig.

The Fleet of the German Reich 1848–1852

National enthusiasm for German unification, kindled by the struggle over Schleswig-Holstein, and practical considerations amongst traders in the Hanseatic towns, led in 1848, the year of the revolution, to the founding of the first navy representing all the German states. For the war which had been waged against Denmark in Schleswig since the beginning of April by Prussia, on behalf of the German Federation, showed that, because of the paucity of their own naval defences, the whole external trade of the German ports on the North and Baltic Seas could easily be blocked by a few Danish warships. A single Danish frigate off Heligoland captured a large number of the trading ships calling at ports on the Weser and Elbe.

The National Assembly at Frankfurt formed a naval committee immediately after it opened, and on 14th July allocated six million thalers for the foundation of a German national military fleet. The Adminis-trator of the Reich elected by the Assembly, Archduke John of Austria, appointed Senator Duckwitz of Bremen Minister of Commerce for the Reich. The latter took over the navy department of the national government and organized the creation of the fleet, so vociferously demanded by the public. Money was raised from all over Germany for that purpose.

On 23rd July, on the initiative of the Hamburg shipowners Godeffroy and Sloman of the Hanseatic Steam Navigation Company, at the request of the Hamburg Admiralty and using the money raised by the naval association founded in April, four trading ships were purchased: the paddle-steamers *Bremen*, *Hamburg* and *Lübeck* and the sailing frigate *Deutschland*. Bremerhaven was designated the base for the Reich's new navy. On 15th October 1848 the "Hamburg Flotilla" entered harbour there; at the beginning of 1849 there followed three ships which Duckwitz had built in England: *Inka*, *Cacique* and *Cora*, which were now called *Grossherzog von Oldenburg*, *Frankfurt* and *König Ernst August;* in addition the Danish frigate *Gefion*, which became *Eckernförde,* was included in the fleet. In March 1849 the North Atlantic steamers *Britannia* and *Acadia,* purchased from the Cunard Line, were added, and they were rechristened *Barbarossa* and *Erzherzog Johann.* In August the *Hansa,* formerly *United States,* sailed into Bremerhaven from America. So the first German navy consisted in the end of three paddle-steamers, six paddle corvettes and two sailing frigates.

The Commander-in-Chief of the fleet was Commander (later Rear-Admiral) Brommy, who had served in the Greek navy. He set up seamanship training in Bremerhaven, subsequently organized the equipping and manning of the ships and then successfully trained the crews of the infant navy.

Left: Paddle frigate *Erzherzog Johann* and frigate *Deutschland* of the fleet of the German Reich.

The lithograph reproduced above shows the Danish ship of the line *Christian VIII* exploding after coming under fire from the shore-battery at Eckernförde, which was occupied by soldiers from Schleswig-Holstein and Nassau. The Danes capitulated—the frigate *Gefion* (left background), which had taken part in the battle, was taken over by the Schleswig-Holsteiners and handed over to the Reich fleet, which was in the course of formation at Bremerhaven.

The *Gefion,* shown above in a contemporary watercoloured pen-and-ink drawing, was launched on 27th September 1843 from the New Royal Shipyard at Copenhagen for the Danish Navy. She was carvel-built of oak clad with copper, and displaced 1300 GRT; she was 59 m long, 13.5 m beam, had a top speed of 15 knots and was equipped with two 60-pounder cannon, and 26 long and 20 short 24-pounder cannon. After the disbandment of the Reich fleet, in which she bore the name *Eckernförde,* she returned again as the *Gefion* to Prussia on 11th May 1852, made many for-

eign voyages as a training ship, became an artillery training ship in 1864, then a floating barracks in Kiel in 1870. Ten years later she was a coal hulk, and was finally broken up in 1891 in the Imperial Shipyard in Kiel. In the picture she flies the black, red and gold flag, the colours of the Reich chosen by the National Assembly. These colours, together with the double-headed black eagle of the Reich, constituted the war flag flown by the German fleet.

The painting on the right, dating from this period, which is in the Fokke-Museum in Bremen, is an expression of the stirring

national consciousness of those times: on the bow of a ship called *Vaterland,* whose figurehead is the old double-headed eagle of the Reich, stands Germania, symbol both of the tradition of the old Reich and of the striving towards unification of the revolutionary years; in the background lie the ships of the Reich's navy. It is a work of originality, full of patriotic zeal for Germany. Its counterpart is the famous freedom figure flourishing the tricolour in Delacroix's painting, "Liberty Leading the People", which dates from the year of the Paris revolution, 1830.

The contemporary lithograph below shows the ships of the Hamburg Flotilla of the German Reich navy in August 1848 on the Elbe at Hamburg. They fly the black, red and gold Reich flag with the eagle.

In the centre foreground lies the sailing frigate *Deutschland*. She was 853 GRT, 38.5 m long, was equipped with 36 cannon, and had a crew of 230 men. At the time when she was taken into the fleet she was already about thirty years old and, like the other Hamburg ships, had to be rebuilt and repaired during the winter of 1848/49 for her new role. At the auction of the fleet in 1852 she was acquired for 9 200 thalers by the Bremen firm of Roessingh & Mummy

for carrying coal from England to China. The paddle corvettes shown in the picture are the *Lübeck*, left background; behind her, the *Bremen*; and on the right the *Hamburg*. All three were smaller paddle-steamers, carvel-built in wood and rigged as schooner brigs. The *Hamburg*, 435 GRT, in 1841 at Bernhard Wencke's yard in Bremen, and was 53 m long with a 12 m beam. The *Bremen* was launched at the Johann Marbs shipyard in Altona as the *Leeds* on 22nd June 1842, measuring 56 m in length, 12.7 m in beam, and displacing 450 GRT. The *Lübeck* was built as *Robert Napier* in 1844 by the firm of S. H. Morton & Co. in Leith, displaced 435 GRT and was 50 m

long by 12.6 m beam. The steamers each had two paddle-wheels 6 m in diameter, each with 12 paddles, and two horizontal one-cylinder expansion engines. They were each equipped with a carronade fore and aft, and two before and behind the paddle-box. Their conversion for use in the fleet was completed on 15th December 1848; in December 1852 they were sold to the General Steam Navigation Co. in London, *Bremen* being renamed *Hanover*, *Hamburg* becoming *Denmark* and *Lübeck* becoming *Newcastle*.

On the right behind the *Deutschland* lies the twelve-gun sailing corvette *Franklin*, which was not taken into the Reich's navy.

The upper picture shows the paddle-wheeled corvette *Hamburg* and the sailing frigate *Deutschland* passing Cuxhaven during their transfer to Bremerhaven, the base of the Reich fleet, in October 1848.

On the right is a wood engraving of the scene on the deck of the *Deutschland* during her auction in Brake by Hannibal Fischer on 18th August 1852.

The preceding double page shows the assembled Reich fleet on the roads at Bremerhaven, from a painting by L. Arenhold which hangs in Schönebeck Castle at Bremen-Vegesack. The paddle-wheeled ships are, from left to right, the frigates *Barbarossa* and *Erzherzog Johann*, the corvettes *Der Königliche Ernst-August* and *Frankfurt*, the frigate *Hansa*, and the corvettes *Bremen*, *Lübeck* and *Hamburg;* on the right are the sailing frigates *Eckernförde* and *Deutschland* of the Hamburg flotilla.

The illustrations below show scenes on board the sailing frigate *Deutschland*. From left to right and from top to bottom: companion way to the forecastle; helmsmen; hammocks on the battery deck; the battery deck; officers on the upper deck; lower deck living quarters.

The only battle waged by the navy of the Reich was a modest attempt by Brommy to put to sea with the frigate *Barbarossa* and the corvettes *Hamburg* and *Lübeck*. To the east of Heligoland he came across a Danish blockade vessel, the sailing corvette *Valkyrien*. There was a little shooting on both sides; it is not known for sure whether either scored a hit against the other. *Valkyrien* withdrew to waters near three other Danish warships lying off Heligoland and the English, who at the time owned Heligoland, fired some shots to warn the warring parties that they were on neutral territory. Brommy retreated to Cuxhaven and two nights later succeeded in reaching Bremerhaven unmolested by the Danes.

The picture above portrays the encounter: in the foreground the *Barbarossa*, on the right the *Hamburg*, in the centre *Valkyrien* and on the left, near the cliffs of Heligoland, the other Danish ships.

Barbarossa was launched as the *Britannia* by the Cunard Line in 1840 and made 99 round trips from Liverpool to Boston before she was acquired by the German fleet and reached Bremerhaven in March 1849. In June 1852 she was taken over by Prussia, was first a residential and guard ship in Danzig, then used as living quarters in Kiel.

One of *Barbarossa's* sister ships was the *Acadia*, built by John Wood in Glasgow in 1839/40 for the Cunard Line. As *Erzherzog Johann* she was acquired for the Reich's navy and, after being stranded at Terschelling during the crossing, sailed into the Weser in March 1849. Four years later she was sold to the shipping firm of W. A. Fritze & Co. in Bremen and renamed *Germania*, put by this firm into Atlantic service on the Bre-

merhaven-New York run, chartered as a British trooper during the Crimean war in 1855 and broken up on the Thames in 1857.

Both ships displaced 1135 GRT, measured 64.7 m, with a 16.5 m beam, and could travel at about 9 knots. They were oak-built, rigged as barques, though the *Barbarossa* was rigged as a brig after 1852. Each of the 9-m diameter paddle-wheels had 24 paddles, driven by two engines built by the Glasgow firm of Napier.

The painting reproduced above, of the German fleet anchored on the Weser, dates from 1850. It shows on the left the sailing frigate *Deutschland,* next to her the paddle-corvettes *Hamburg, Bremen* and *Lübeck,* one behind the other, and in the right foreground the paddle-wheeled frigate *Hansa.*

Hansa, about 1800 GRT, was the largest ship in the fleet. She was launched in 1847 as the *United States* by the Black Ball Line for the North Atlantic run, and had made four round trips across the Atlantic before she was purchased by the German fleet. She entered the Weser in August 1849. In March 1853 she was sold to the Bremen shipping firm W. A. Fritze & Co. for whom, with an interruption of service during which she was chartered as a British trooper in the Crimean war, she was employed on the Atlantic Bremerhaven-New York run until 1857. After that, she was chartered for British transport to India and finally sold to the English Galway Line, for which she sailed to India from 1858 onwards as the *Indian Empire.* In July 1862 she was gutted by fire in Deptford.

The 1850 painting reproduced below, from the collection of Dr. Jobst in Bremen, also shows the flagship *Hansa* in the background. In the foreground lies the only two-funnelled steamer in the fleet, the paddle-wheeled corvette *Grossherzog von Oldenburg*. Except for the second funnel she differs little from her single-funnelled sister ships *Der Königliche Ernst August* and *Frankfurt,* with which she was commissioned from the W. M. Petterson shipyard in Bristol by Duckwitz, the Minister of Commerce for the Reich. All three steamers arrived at Bremerhaven in spring 1849. During construction they bore code names, out of consideration for British neutrality. They were carvel-built with oak transverse ribs and yellow pine planking, had two horizontal expansion engines, and were driven by two paddle-wheels measuring 5.5 m in diameter and having twelve paddles each. In December 1852 they were auctioned in Brake to the General Steam Navigation Co. of London. The *Grossherzog von Oldenburg* displaced 600 GRT, was 50.3 m long with a beam of 14.8 m, and equipped with two 68-pound carronades. Her original code-name was *Inca,* her later name *Belgium*. *Der Königliche Ernst August* was a ship of 900 GRT, 55.5 m long, 17.1 m beam, armed with six 68-pound carronades. She was originally called *Cora* and later *Edinburgh*. The *Frankfurt* displaced 625 GRT, measured 51 m long by 14.4 m beam, and was first called *Cazique,* then *Holland*. All three ships could reach about 9 knots; *Der Königliche Ernst-August* had a crew of 5 officers and 145 men, the others had 4 officers and 96 men each.

The lithograph reproduced above, which is
in the possession of the German Ship
Museum in Bremerhaven, dates from 1849
and shows (from left to right) *Hansa*,
Deutschland, *Frankfurt* and *Barbarossa* anchored off Bremerhaven, which is in the
background.

By the time the complete fleet had been equipped and armed and its crews fully trained—towards the end of 1849—the public enthusiasm which had run high a year earlier had vanished. The Revolution had run aground; the National Assembly and the acting national government as well were awaiting dissolution; a final ceasefire had been arrived at with Denmark; and the aim of German unification remained unfulfilled.

For three years the ships lay idle on the Weser, the bigger ones at Bremerhaven, the smaller *Hamburg, Lübeck, Bremen* and *Grossherzog von Oldenburg* at Brake. At length Parliament elected Dr. Hannibal Fischer, a rather unfortunate choice, to be the fleet's Federal Commissioner, with instructions to disband it. *Barbarossa* and *Eckernförde* (which latter reverted to her former name, *Gefion*) were taken over by Prussia, while Fischer auctioned off the others in Bremerhaven and Brake, together with all the naval stores.

BREMER POST DAMPFSCHIFF
·HANSA·

Länge 262 Fuís. Breite 70 Fuís.   2200 Tons groís 2 Maschinen von 1000 Pferdekraft

The watercolour above belongs to the Ship
Museum of the Oldenburg Weser ports, in
Brake, and shows the *Hansa*, the largest
ship in the first German fleet. She plied the
Atlantic after being sold to the Bremen
shipping firm of Fritze.

Right: the Prussian cadet training ship
Arcona, a painting by Max Schröder-
Greifswald owned by the Mürwik Naval
College (see page 35).

The provisional government of Schleswig-Holstein had also established its own fleet in 1848 in order to resist the Danish blockade. It consisted of 11 oar-propelled gunboats each with two carronades; the paddle-wheeled tug *Löwe*, which was armed with one gun; the packet-boat *Bonin* with its four cannon; and the requisitioned Danish schooner *Elbe*, which was used as a training ship for the cadet school that had been set up in Kiel. These ships too flew the black, red and gold national flag with the eagle on the jack.

The lithograph of 1850 reproduced on the next page shows the fleet in Kiel harbour: on the horizon the tug *Löwe*, in the centre the *Elbe* and in the right foreground the steamer *Bonin*. The *Bonin* managed to force the withdrawal of the Danish steamer *Hekla* when she launched an attack in the Kiel Bight in June 1849. The gunboats carried out some small and partly successful operations on the Baltic and North Sea coasts. On the left of the picture in the foreground is the steam-propelled gunboat *Von der Tann*, the first German warship to be screw-driven. During an encounter with the Danish ships *Valkyrien* and *Hekla* off Neustadt she ran aground and was set alight by the crew to avoid her capture.

Above is a reproduction of a painting by Alex Kircher, which is now in the Mürwik Naval College. It shows the Prussian ships *Loreley* (left, see page 44), behind her *Nymphe* (see page 44) and *Arcona* (centre, see pages 29 and 34) during the sea battle off Jasmund in 1864.

The illustration on the right is a painting by L. Arenhold, showing the Prussian fleet in 1854. From left to right: the despatch-boats *Salamander* and *Nix*, the flagship *Danzig;* the *Gefion, Hela* and *Amazone,* and behind them the *Barbarossa* and *Mercur,* which were taken over from the fleet of the Reich.

Prussian and Austrian Warships 1848–1866

After the fleet of the Reich had been disbanded, Austria and Prussia were the only German states to retain warships. The black, gold and red flag, symbol of a democratic unified German Reich, had been struck. The German provinces again flew their own colours exclusively: Prussia the black eagle on a white background, Austria the red, white and red flag with the Austrian coat of arms.

Nevertheless, events in Schleswig-Holstein had made people in both states aware of the importance of having one's own effective warships. Two seafaring princes from the ruling houses soon came forward to take over the command of the newly-created central administration of the fleet. The first Prussian Admiral was Prince Adalbert, who was appointed head of the Admiralty established in 1853. In Austria in the same year, Archduke Ferdinand Max,

brother of the Emperor Franz Joseph and later Emperor of Mexico, became the Commander-in-Chief of the Navy, taking the rank of Vice-Admiral. In March 1848 in Venice there had been a successful mutiny of the Italian crews of the Austrian ships, which was put down in the summer. The result of this was a reorganization of the fleet under German-speaking command. Pola replaced Venice as the new base. Both princes initiated and sponsored foreign voyages for ships which served not only for training and display but which were more and more frequently carrying out important research assignments.

Prince Adalbert of Prussia himself had a share in the design of the two swift paddle-driven despatch-boats *Nix* and *Salamander*, both of 530 GRT. They were built in 1850 by Robinson and Russell of London and could reach 13 knots. But they were a

failure. In 1855, in a deal with the British Admiralty, they were exchanged for the training frigate *Thetis*. November 1851 saw the launching of the first home-built larger Prussian warship, the paddle-corvette *Danzig*, from the Royal Shipyards in Danzig. She was a carvel-built oak ship of 1200 GRT, overlaid with copper, almost 76 m long and with a top speed of over 11 knots. Equipped with twelve 68-pounder British carronades, she became the Prince's first flagship. From her decks in 1856 the Prince carried out the landing against the Riff pirates at Tres Forcas.

After making some foreign voyages, the *Danzig* was first sold in 1863 to England and then to Japan, where she was burnt out in 1869. In 1854 the schooner *Helga*, constructed in the Royal Shipyards at Danzig, was put into service as a training ship (see page 61).

Five wooden frigates of similar type were built mainly for foreign voyages between 1855 and 1869: *Arcona, Gazelle, Vineta, Hertha* and *Elisabeth*, the first Prussian warships with screw propellers. *Arcona* was 1527 GRT in weight, 72 m long, 13 m beam, could do a good 12 knots and was fitted with six 68-pounder and twenty 36-pounder cannon. She sailed abroad a great deal, taking part in 1869 in the opening of the Suez Canal, with the Prussian Crown Prince on board; and when surprised by the enemy in the Azores in 1870, succeeded in avoiding contact with the French ships which outnumbered her, and making her way through to Lisbon. In 1867 she was broken up in Kiel. In 1859–62 she joined the *Thetis* and the schooner *Frauenlob*, built in 1855, on a Far Eastern tour to China and Japan. On 2nd September 1860,

in Japanese waters, the *Frauenlob* fell victim to a typhoon, from which *Arcona* herself only narrowly escaped. *Frauenlob* was built at the Lübke shipyard in Wolgast between 1849 and 1856 with money raised in a charitable collection started by German women throughout the country in 1848, the year of the revolution. She was carvel-built in wood, 94 GRT, 32 m long, and could cruise at 13 knots. She had a crew of 5 officers and 42 men, all of whom went down with the ship. The schooner *Helga* (see page 61) was a similar type to the *Frauenlob*.

The woodcut below, dated 1860, shows the *Arcona* on the left, the *Thetis* in the centre, and the *Frauenlob* on the right. The woodcut above right depicts the Crossing the Line ceremony, always a lively event, on board the *Arcona* during her homeward voyage in 1861.

The despatch-boat *Grille,* pictured right, destined to be the Prussian royal yacht, was launched by the Normand Shipyard in Le Havre in September 1857. In 1870 she withstood an attack by French naval forces near Rügen. She was later rebuilt several times and served as a training ship from 1892 onwards, becoming the most long-lived ship of the German navy. In 1920 she was scrapped in Hamburg. She was carvel-built in mahogany, 326 GRT, was almost 57 m long and, rigged as a three-mast schooner and, fitted with a British single-expansion engine, could do 13 knots.

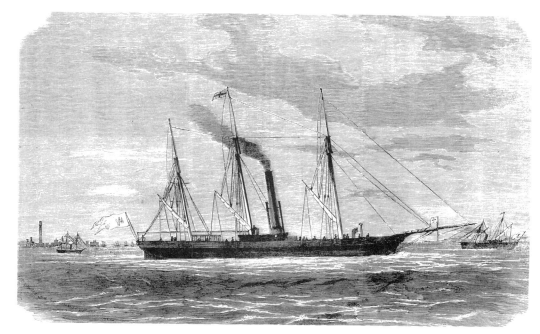

At the instigation of the Archduke Ferdinand Max, the Austrian sailing frigate *Novara,* which was launched in Venice in 1850, sailed round the world. This was the first significant scientific expedition made by a German warship and at the same time it served as a training exercise in seamanship for the potential officers on board. From Trieste via Gibraltar she crossed the Atlantic to Rio, and from there around the Cape of Good Hope into the Indian Ocean. She put in at various islands, St. Paul, Ceylon, the Nicobar Islands and Java, and at each of them the crew undertook research expeditions inland. The ship returned to Trieste on 26th August 1859, having travelled via Shanghai, Australia, New Zealand, the Pacific, and then Valparaiso.

The wood engravings reproduced here give an impression of life on board during the voyage: above a crew "ball" on deck; above right, divine service; below right, the mess used by officers and the scientists who joined them for the trip.

Above is the arrival of the *Novara* in Trieste harbour. The *Novara* is on the left, followed by the steam yacht *Fantasie,* the frigate *Adria* and another frigate.

During these years Austria invested somewhat more than Prussia in ship-building. By 1857 Austria had a squadron in service, consisting of the four screw-propelled frigates *Adria, Donau, Erzherzog Friedrich* and *Dandolo.* In Pola in 1860 the ship of the line *Kaiser* was launched, in 1862/63 the armoured frigates *Don Juan, Kaiser Max,* *Prinz Eugen, Ferdinand Max* and *Habsburg* were completed, and the existing sailing frigates, amongst them *Novara* and *Schwarzenberg,* were converted to screw propulsion.

The woodcut left shows the Austrian ship-of-the-line *Kaiser* after her commissioning in 1860. She was built of wood, had a displacement of 5 194 t and took part in 1866 in the victorious battle of Lissa led by Admiral Tegethoff. The *Kaiser* was the only wooden sailing battleship that the Austrian navy ever owned.

Between 1859 and 1865 Prussia had her first steam-driven gunboats built at various shipyards in Stettin, Danzig, Wolgast and Elbing. Until then gunboats had been rowing-boats, either yawls or sloops. Two new types of gunboats were built; the so-called First or Chameleon Class, 203 GRT, were 43 m long, had four officers, a crew of 67, could make a good 9 knots and were equipped with one 24-pound and two 12-pound cannon. The Second or Hunting Class, 164 GRT, were 41 m long and armed in the same way as ships of the Chameleon Class. There were fifteen ships in the Hunting Class, one of which is pictured below, but they were seldom in service.

Of the total of 8 ships in the Chameleon Class, only the *Delphin, Blitz, Basilisk, Meteor* and *Drache* were employed in the dual role of foreign service and as survey ships.

The *Niobe*, launched from the Royal Dockyard in Portsmouth in 1849, was a similar type of ship to the *Thetis*, which was exchanged for *Nix* and *Salamander*. She was bought by the Prussian navy in 1861 and used for training cadets before being finally broken up in Kiel in 1891.

The picture above is a photograph (1883) of the *Niobe* at anchor in Dartmouth harbour during a training voyage. She displaced 854 GRT, could do 14 knots and had a sail area of 1650 sqm; she was equipped with sixteen 68-pounder and four 30-pounder cannon.

The *Thetis*, 1082 GRT, had a sail area of 2370 sqm, and could do up to 15 knots. She too was a cadet training ship, later a gunnery training ship, and was scrapped in 1895 in Kiel. The crews of both ships comprised 35 officers and 320 men.

Above is a contemporary woodcut showing the visit of the Prussian warships to Hamburg on 3rd September 1861.

Arcona (see page 34), the first screw-propelled frigate of the Prussian navy, was followed up to 1869 by four similar ships, *Gazelle* (see page 64), *Vineta, Hertha* (see page 65) and *Elisabeth*. They all had a sail area of about 2200 sqm and could do 12 knots.

The woodcut on the right shows, from left to right, the Prussian warships *Musquito, Niobe, Arcona, Rover* and *Nymphe* in 1864 on the roadstead at Swinemünde. *Musquito* and *Rover* were cadet training ships built in 1851 and 1853 in England.

The *Vineta*, pictured right, was launched in 1863 by J. Penn & Sons of Greenwich, was 73 m long and armed with twenty-eight 68-pounder cannon.

Below is a lithograph of 1864 showing the Prussian screw-driven corvette *Vineta*, in the foreground, the schooner *Hela* on the left and on the right the *Delphin*, one of the Chameleon or First Class steam-driven gunboats built between 1859 and 1860 at the Royal Shipyards in Danzig.

The paddle-wheeled despatch-boat *Loreley*, launched by the Royal Shipyards in Danzig in 1859, was of modest dimensions: 290 GRT and 47 m long. She served the same purpose, however—mostly foreign voyages—as the flush-decked corvettes *Nymphe* and *Medusa*, which were considerably bigger. Each of them was 728 GRT and 65 m long. They had single-expansion engines by J. Penn & Sons of Greenwich, ten 36-pounder and six 12-pounder cannon and a sail area of 1500 sqm.

Nymphe was launched on 15th April 1863 in Danzig and sailed foreign waters. In 1870 she took part in the sea battle at Jasmund and in 1870 successfully prevented the invasion of Danzig by a French squadron. Until 1885 she again voyaged abroad, then was stationed in Kiel and in 1891 was broken up in Hamburg.

Medusa also made many trips abroad; during the Franco-Prussian war she sought refuge in Yokohama harbour from superior French naval forces. In 1891 she was scrapped in Danzig. The picture at right is the *Medusa* in 1872.

The *Augusta* and *Viktoria* were also flush-decked corvettes with screw propulsion. They were built in 1863/64 by L'Arman Frères in Bordeaux. They were originally ordered by the southern States during the Civil War, then were purchased by Japan under the names *Jeddon* and *Osakka*, but were not accepted after launching. Prussia acquired them in May 1864 and put them into service on 3rd July 1864. They were carvel-built, wooden flush-decked corvettes, with a sail area of 1600 sqm. The *Augusta*, named after the Queen of Prussia, was equipped with eight 24-pounder and 6 long 12-pounder guns, had an overall length of 81.5 m, a maximum beam of 11.1 m and a draught of 5.03 m. Her two-cylinder expansion engine originated from Mazeline in Le Havre and gave her a top speed of 13.5 knots. The crew consisted of 15 officers and 215 non-commissioned officers and men. In the Franco-Prussian war she was the only German ship brought in to disrupt trade. In this capacity the *Augusta* succeeded in stopping a brig, a barque and a government steamer belonging to the enemy, at the mouth of the Gironde in 1871. She then put into the northern Spanish port of Vigo, where she was trapped by a blockade of French warships until the ceasefire. On the last of her numerous voyages overseas, she was lost with all her crew in the Gulf of Aden on 2nd June 1885. She had been on her way to Australia and had probably fallen victim to a hurricane.

The picture above shows the *Augusta* after her commissioning in 1864 on the roadsteads outside Bremerhaven.

In 1864 Schleswig-Holstein was again the subject of war against Denmark. Prussian and Austrian troops waged a successful campaign in Schleswig. To begin with the Prussian fleet was deployed alone against the Danes and was too weak to prevent a blockade of the Baltic and North Sea ports. At the outbreak of war, the steamships ready for action were the corvettes *Arcona*, *Gazelle*, *Vineta* and *Nymphe*, the frigate *Barbarossa*, the despatch-boats *Preussischer Adler* and *Loreley*, the yacht *Grille* and 21 gunboats. In addition there were the sailing ships *Gefion*, *Thetis*, *Niobe*, *Musquito* and *Rover*, as well as three schooners and 40 armed sloops and yawls.

The fleet massed in Swinemünde. On 15th March the Danish blockade of the Pomeranian coast began. During a reconnaissance trip made by Captain Jachmann from Swinemünde to Rügen, the Prussian ships *Arcona*, *Nymphe* and *Loreley* met and fought an indecisive two-hour battle against superior Danish naval forces at Jasmund (see page 32). This showed, nonetheless, that the Prussian fleet could defend her own Baltic coasts—though, when it came to the North Sea, the Prussians had to rely on help from the Austrians.

For this reason an Austrian squadron, including the frigates *Schwarzenberg* and *Radetzky* and the gunboat *Seehund*, sailed from the Mediterranean to the North Sea under the command of Captain Tegethoff. On the way, at Brest, they joined up with the Prussian ships *Preussischer Adler*, *Blitz* and *Basilisk*, which were returning from voyages abroad. The *Novara*, the ship of the line *Kaiser*, the armoured frigate *Don Juan d'Austria*, the corvette *Erzherzog Friedrich*, the gunboat *Wall*, and the paddle-steamer *Kaiserin Elisabeth* as despatch-boat, were to follow under the command of Rear-Admiral von Wüllerstorff-Urbair. On 9th May battle was joined between Tegethoff's squadron and the three Danish frigates, *Jylland*, *Niels Juel* and *Heimdall*, off the coast of Heligoland. The Danes managed to set *Schwarzenberg* alight and then, after Tegethoff had retreated into the neutral English waters of Heligoland, left the scene of battle. As a result, the Danish blockade of the mouths of the Elbe and Weser was lifted and Tegethoff's ships put into Cuxhaven, which Baron von Wüllerstorff-Urbair and his division of the fleet reached only at the beginning of July. Until the ceasefire, the combined Austrian North Sea fleet then guaranteed unhindered passage in and out of North German harbours. The fleet is shown in the contemporary woodcut below.

The ships depicted are (from left to right): *Schwarzenberg*, *Don Juan d'Austria*, *Radetzky*, *Seehund*, *Kaiser*, *Wall*, *Erzherzog Friedrich* and *Kaiserin Elisabeth*.

The wood engraving below, taken from the *Leipziger Illustrierte* of 1864, shows the Austro-Prussian squadron under Tegethoff entering Cuxhaven after the sea fight off Heligoland. In the foreground is the Cuxhaven lighthouse with the mole known as *"Alte Liebe"* (dear old lady), on the left the *Schwarzenberg* with its foremast reduced to a stump in the course of the battle, and on the right the Prussian gunboats.

The above picture of the fight off Heligoland is reproduced from one of the Neuruppin Picture Sheets, which were very popular at the time, now in the Shipping Museum at Brake. Seen in the background are the Danish steam frigates *Niels Juel, Jylland* and *Heimdal,* one behind the other, firing on the Austrian ships in the foreground, *Radetzky* and *Schwarzenberg* (with her foremast on fire) and on the Prussian despatch-boat *Preussischer Adler* and gunboats *Blitz* and *Basilisk,* on the right. It was the last engagement to be fought between large warships built exclusively of wood.

The artist was clearly not well versed in naval matters, as the colours of the Austrian ships' flags are wrongly depicted on the Picture Sheet: instead of black, yellow and black, they should have been red, white and red, with the Austrian coat of arms in the middle of the flag.

The Fleet of the North German Federation 1867–1871

After the victory over Denmark, during which Schleswig-Holstein was ceded to the allied forces, disputes arose between Austria and Prussia which led to war in 1866. Austria, which was at that time also engaged in a war with Italy, succeeded in mustering almost her entire fleet and gained a victory over the Italians at Lissa, in spite of the superior strength of the mobilized Italian ships. However, in the course of her war with Prussia, lasting only six weeks, there were no encounters between naval forces.

The struggle was decided by the defeat of the Austrian army at Königgrätz; Prussia retained not only Schleswig-Holstein and Hannover, but also the major part of the German North Sea coast, as well as the Baltic port of Kiel, which since 1865 had been a base for the Prussian naval operations and was her most important naval station. A

new Prussian naval base on the North Sea was established on a site on Jade Bay which had been captured from Oldenburg in 1854. The German Federation, to which all German states including Austria had belonged, was dissolved; from then on Germany's development took place without Austria—and the same was true also of the future German navy.

Under the leadership of Prussia, the north German states joined the North German Federation and Prussia's fleet became the Fleet of the North German Federation. From 1st October 1867 onwards, its ships flew the black, white and red flag, a combination of the black and white colours of Prussia and the red and white of the Hanseatic towns.

The illustration above shows the former Prussian ships (from left to right) *Gefion*,

Niobe, *Thetis*, *Nymphe* and *Arcona* as part of the Fleet of the North German Federation in 1867 in the Baltic.

A plan for the creation of the Federation's fleet was drawn up, aiming at the following strength ten years later: 16 armoured ships, 20 frigates and corvettes, 8 despatch-boats, 22 steam-driven gunboats, 2 artillery ships and 5 training ships. On 15th June 1869 the naval harbour in Jade Bay was inaugurated and received the name of Wilhelmshaven.

The Prussian navy had already put some smaller armoured vessels into service, the first being the London-built monitor *Arminius*, in 1865, and the second the *Prinz Adalbert*, built by L'Arman Frères in Bordeaux, in 1866. The *Prinz Adalbert* was also the first twin-screw ship in the Prussian fleet. Subsequently the first three armoured frigates were commissioned for the German Federation from France and England. *Friedrich Carl,* a second-rate battery ship, was built by the Compagnie des Forges et Chantiers in Toulon. As in *Prinz Adalbert* and *Arminius,* the ship's ribs were made of iron and her planking from teak, armoured with wrought iron. *Friedrich Carl* (see illustration on page 55) was 94 m long, had a displacement of 5971 t, had a single-expansion engine and, rigged as a barque with 2010 sqm of sail, easily reached a speed of 13 knots. The crew consisted of 33 officers and about 500 men. After 25 years of service in the fleet the *Friedrich Carl* became a torpedo trials ship in 1892 and in 1906 was sold to Holland for scrap.

The next armoured frigate, also a second-rate battery ship, was the *Kronprinz,* completed by Samuda Brothers of London on 6th May 1867. She was almost 90 m long, displaced 5767 t, also had a single-expansion engine, and when rigged as a barque had a sail area of 1980 sqm. Her crew strength was the same as that of the *Friedrich Carl* and she was similarly equipped, though with thirty-two 72-pounder rifled guns (of which *Friedrich Carl* had only 26). The *Kronprinz* remained in service until 1901, then became a hulk in Kiel, and was finally broken up in Rendsburg.

The picture at top right shows her launching at the docks in Poplar; in the centre picture she is seen in her completed state in 1867.

The third armoured frigate, a first-rate battery ship, was built at the Thames Iron Works in Blackwall. Originally planned as the Turkish ship *Fatikh,* she was purchased during construction and was launched on 25th April 1868 as the *König Wilhelm.* She had a displacement of 9757 t and was 112 m long. She had an expansion engine and when fully-rigged, with a sail area of 2600 sqm, could make almost 15 knots. She was armed with thirty-three 72-pounder cannon. She joined the service in 1869, then after a major reconstruction by Blohm & Voss in Hamburg was classified, from early 1897 onwards, as a large cruiser. She was laid up in 1904, then used as living and training quarters in Kiel and Mürwik, and was broken up in 1921.

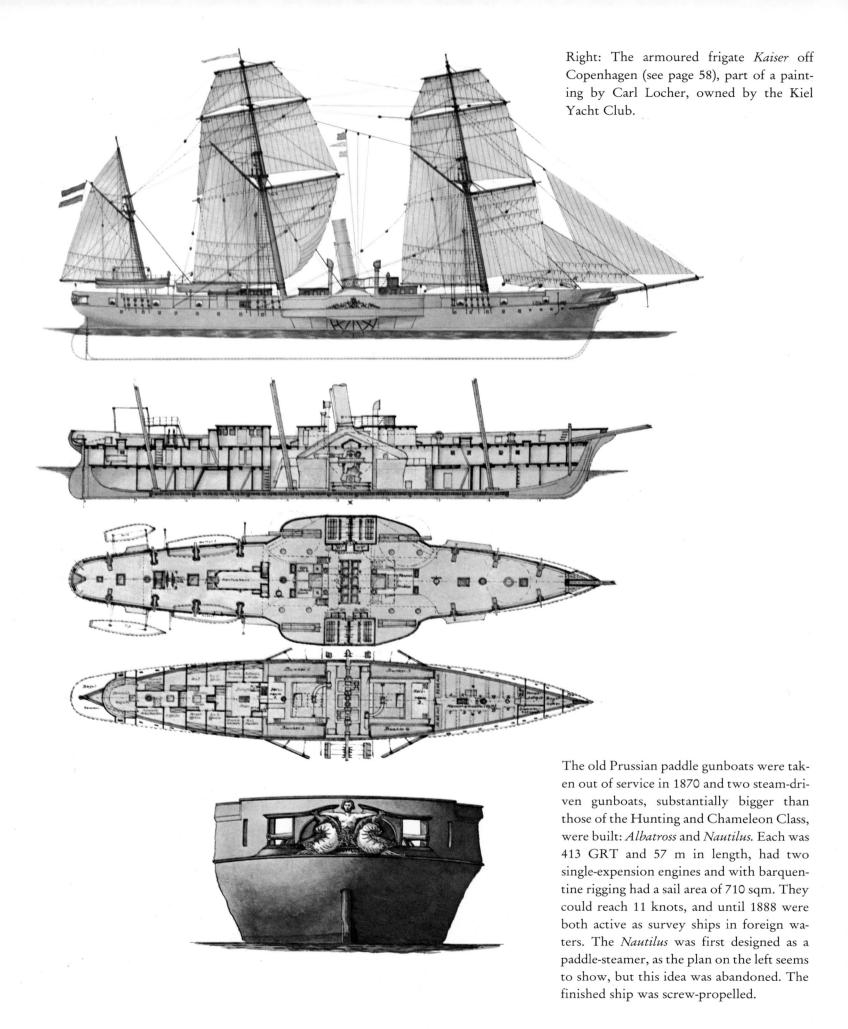

Right: The armoured frigate *Kaiser* off Copenhagen (see page 58), part of a painting by Carl Locher, owned by the Kiel Yacht Club.

The old Prussian paddle gunboats were taken out of service in 1870 and two steam-driven gunboats, substantially bigger than those of the Hunting and Chameleon Class, were built: *Albatross* and *Nautilus*. Each was 413 GRT and 57 m in length, had two single-expension engines and with barquentine rigging had a sail area of 710 sqm. They could reach 11 knots, and until 1888 were both active as survey ships in foreign waters. The *Nautilus* was first designed as a paddle-steamer, as the plan on the left seems to show, but this idea was abandoned. The finished ship was screw-propelled.

The Imperial Navy 1871–1888

In the Franco-Prussian war of 1870/71 there were no noteworthy attacks by the much superior French fleet on the German fleet or the German coast: as in the 1864 war with Denmark, it was the army which, with remarkable speed, won the decisive victory. As mentioned earlier, *Nymphe* made a minor attack on French ships forming a blockade outside Danzig, and *Augusta* captured a few smallish trading vessels at the mouth of the Gironde. There was in addition a brief struggle between the gunboat *Meteor,* which belonged to the Hunting Class, and the French despatch-boat *Bouvet,* near Havana.

After the founding of the Reich in January 1871 at Versailles, the Fleet of the North German Federation became the Imperial Navy, the fleet of the Reich. It was put under the supreme command of Prussia, in the person of Kaiser Wilhelm I. The former Navy Ministry was renamed the "Imperial Admiralty" in 1872 and its first head was General von Stosch.

This Imperial Navy had no ambition, in the first decades, to compete with the great ocean-going fleets such as those of England or even of France. Defence of the coasts and protection of German sea trade were its main concerns, according to a memorandum drafted by Stosch.

He planned that there should be two foreign bases, in Eastern Asia and in the West Indies, each to be occupied by two corvettes and a gunboat. A further "flying" foreign squadron should include an armoured frig-
ate, two corvettes and a gunboat, and should have in reserve three armoured frigates, three corvettes and two gunboats. The main forces, however, were to ensure the security of the coasts; here there were to be eight armoured frigates in the North Sea and six in the Baltic. All in all the idea was that of a defensive fleet, and its construction was immediately and speedily begun. The aim was to add the following ships by 1882 to the ships already in existence and those already planned: eight armoured frigates, six armoured corvettes, seven armoured monitors, 20 unarmoured corvette cruisers, 6 despatch-boats, 18 gunboats, 28 torpedo vessels and 5 training ships. These were to make up an effective but purely defensive fleet.

The contemporary wood engraving on the left shows a squadron of the new Imperial Navy on the roads at Danzig. It consists of the armoured frigates *Kronprinz* and, on her right, *Friedrich Carl* and the flush-decked corvette *Ariadne*. The *Kronprinz*, as the flagship, is flying the admiral's flag at the head of the mizzen-mast, and is firing from two ports to starboard.

The picture above shows the German Reich squadron in 1872. From left to right the ships are the *Vineta, Gazelle, Friedrich Carl* (as flagship of the squadron commander, Captain Werner, with the commodore's pennant at the head of the main-mast), *Albatross* and *Elisabeth*.

At the beginning of 1870 the old British screw-driven battleship *Renown* was purchased for use as gunnery training ship (see page 61). The construction of the flush-decked corvette *Ariadne* (pictured left) was begun at the Imperial Shipyard in Danzig in the same year. She was launched in July 1871, was in service from 1872 to 1890, mostly on voyages overseas, and was broken up in Hamburg in 1891. In all technical details, she matched her sister ship *Luise* (see page 66).

A series of protected corvette cruisers was launched at various shipyards from the mid-1870s onwards. These were the *Bismarck, Blücher, Stosch, Moltke, Gneisenau* and *Stein*. They were all fitted with an expansion engine and, fully-rigged, had a sail area of 2210 sqm. These corvettes of the Bismarck Class were designated as third-raters.

The painting reproduced above is by Alex Kircher and shows from left to right *Stosch, Gneisenau* and *Moltke*.

Stosch was launched in October 1877 by A. G. vulcan of Stettin, and was in overseas service until 1886, during which time she took part in the operation in Zanzibar which led to the acquisition of German East Africa. She became a training ship in 1891 and in 1907 was taken out of service and broken up. *Moltke* and *Gneisenau* were both built at the Imperial Shipyard in Danzig, with launchings in October 1877 and September 1879. They too served in foreign parts and were later training ships; *Moltke* was scrapped at Kiel in 1920. Following missions off Cameroon in 1884 and Zanzibar in 1885, *Gneisenau* was lost in a storm off Malaga on 16th December 1900. All 41 crew, amongst them the commanding officer, Captain Kretschmann, lost their lives. The wrecked ship's masts could still be seen towering out of the water many years later.

The ships of the Bismarck Class originally had 18 officers and 386 men, or about 450 men when in use as training ships. *Stosch* and *Moltke* had ten and *Gneisenau* fourteen 15-cm Krupp guns and each ship had in addition two 8.8-cm quick-firing cannon.

The photograph on the right shows the paddle corvette *Preussischer Adler,* which took part in the battle off Heligoland in 1864. She was launched by Dutchburn & Mare of London in 1846 and until her inclusion in the Prussian navy in 1862 plied between Swinemünde and Kronstadt as a mailboat. From 1868 she was the Royal Yacht and it is at this time that the photograph was taken. In 1879 she was blown up during torpedo tests in Kiel.

Below are the *Gefion* and the *Rover,* photographed in the 1870s.

The armoured frigates *Kaiser* and *Deutschland* were two first-rates fitted with casemates; they were launched in 1872 by Bermuda Brothers in Poplar, and were the last of the larger German warships built abroad. They displaced 7600 t, were 89 m long, had single-expansion engines and a sail area of 1623 sqm, fully-rigged, and could maintain a speed of 14.5 knots. They were each equipped with eight 26-cm Krupp cannon and had a crew of 32 officers and 568 men. *Kaiser* was in 1888 the flagship of the squadron, and in her Wilhelm II made his first state voyage to St. Petersburg, Stockholm and Copenhagen (see page 53); both ships were converted in the mid-nineties into large cruisers without rigging, and from 1904 onwards served as harbour ships.

On the right is an impression of the launching of the *Kaiser* at Poplar. On it can be clearly seen the portside casemate. The picture below shows the *Kaiser* after her commissioning in 1875 as a flagship, flying the admiral's flag at the head of the foremast. The flag was that of the head of the Navy, von Stosch, who had been promoted to Admiral that year.

The picture opposite also dates from 1875 and shows ships passing in review before the Emperor and firing salutes. They are, from left to right, the armoured frigates *König Wilhelm*, *Kaiser* and *Kronprinz*, the armoured corvette *Hansa* (see page 68), the despatch-boat *Falke*, built in 1865, and the monitor *Arminius*.

The training ships *Musquito* (left) and *Rover* (below), built in England, are shown here in old photographs from the 1870s. They were launched from the Royal Dockyard in Pembroke in 1851 and 1853 respectively, and were purchased ten years later by the Prussian navy. Rigged as brigs, they were in active service until 1886 and 1890 respectively.

On the right is a photograph, also dating from the seventies, of the training ship *Hela*. In the same way as her sister ship *Frauenlob* was financed by collections amongst German women, so *Hela* was paid for by contributions from Prussian voters in 1848/49. She was launched from the Royal Shipyard and was at first rigged as a topsail schooner, with 523 sqm of sail, and then, after 1860, as a brig, with a sail area of 604 sqm. She carried three heavy and six light 24-pounder cannon and in all other respects was the same as the *Frauenlob*. In 1871 she was taken out of service and scrapped.

Above left is a photograph from the 1870s showing the artillery training ship *Renown* at anchor in Wilhelmshaven. She was one of the earliest ships in the German navy and was moreover the only large wooden ship-of-the-line of the old type that the German fleet had ever owned. She was bought in England in 1870. She was launched at the Royal Dockyard in Portsmouth in 1857 as a second-rate British ship-of-the-line. She was carvel-built, 74 m long, displaced 5 700 t and had a single-expansion engine. Fully-rigged, with 4 500 sqm of sail, she could do 10 knots. She had room on the two battery decks for 91 cannon which came from the British Naval Arsenal at Woolwich. As was customary with the old ships-of-the-line, the ports on these decks were identified by white stripes. *Renown* was acquired by the German fleet for training purposes. She lay in the harbour at Wilhelmshaven, with a crew of 42 officers and 477 men, and was equipped in various ways, either for instruction or tests. She was first a gunnery training ship, then from 1881 onwards living quarters. In 1892, when her usefulness was at an end, she was sold back to England for scrap.

The armoured ships *Preussen* and *Hansa* are pictured above. On the left is the armoured ship *Friedrich der Grosse* at her launching in Kiel on 20th September 1874. She is shown in the illustration on the right after her commissioning.

While the Prusso-German armoured frigates *Kronprinz, Kaiser* and *Deutschland* were English-designed, brainchildren of the construction engineer Sir E. Reed, it was the *Hansa* (see page 68), launched in 1872 at the Imperial Shipyard in Danzig, that was the first armoured ship to be built according to plans developed in the construction division of the navy of the North German Federation. She was an armoured screw-driven corvette, made of iron-clad teak, 73 m long and with a displacement of 3950 t. She was powered by a single-expansion engine, had a sail area of 1760 sqm when fully-rigged, sailed at 13 knots and had a crew of 28 officers and 371 men. She had casemates fitted with eight 21-cm Krupp cannon. On joining the fleet, she spent from 1878 to 1880 in South America, then she was a harbour guard-ship in Kiel.

After 1888 she provided living quarters and in 1906 she was broken up in Swinemünde.

The Reichstag brought pressure to bear on Admiral von Stosch, urging national independence in the building of the fleet. Under von Stosch, therefore, all important new ships were from this time onwards designed in Germany and completed in German shipyards. Similarly, the first German armoured ships with gun turrets were built according to official designs conceived by the Federal navy. These were the three Prussian-Class frigates, 6821 t and measuring 96 m in length: *Preussen* (launched by AG. Vulcan in Stettin in 1873), *Friedrich der Grosse* (launched in 1874 at the Imperial Shipyard in Kiel) and *Grosser Kurfürst* (launched at the Imperial Shipyard in Wilhelmshaven, 1875). Their armour consisted of teak planking clad in

wrought iron. They had German-made single-expansion engines, a crew of 46 officers and 454 men to handle 1834 sqm of sail, under full rigging, and could maintain a speed of 14 knots. *Preussen* was on active service in the fleet until 1891, then became a harbour ship in Wilhelmshaven; was renamed *Saturn* in 1903 after the commissioning of the new battleship *Preussen*, became a coal hulk in 1906, and was scrapped in 1919 in Wilhelmshaven. The same dates apply to the armoured ship *Friedrich der Grosse*, except that she was scrapped a year later in Rönnebeck. Her sister ship *Grosser Kurfürst* collided with the armoured ship *König Wilhelm* during formation exercises in the English Channel off Folkestone as early as 1878, and was lost. Through an oversight the watertight doors were not closed, and the ship sank with 269 men.

The screw-propelled frigate *Gazelle* shown on the left, a sister ship of the *Arcona*, was launched in 1859 at the Royal Shipyard in Danzig and voyaged abroad a great deal. In 1874—76 she circumnavigated the globe, carrying out important scientific investigations, especially in New Guinea, which gave impetus to its acquisition later as a German protectorate.

The *Hertha,* photographed right, was also a sister ship of the *Arcona.* Launched in Danzig in 1864, she too voyaged mostly overseas. On one such voyage, she took part in an action against the West African Kingdom of Dahomey. *Gazelle* and *Hertha* ceased active service in 1884 and served from then until 1902 and 1906 respectively as living quarters and coal hulks.

On the left, in a photograph taken in the 1870s, is the armoured frigate *Kronprinz.*

The photograph on the left shows flush-decked corvette *Nymphe,* sister ship to the *Medusa,* during one of her numerous foreign voyages, in a Mediterranean harbour. In 1871—75 she travelled around the world.

These full-rigged corvettes driven by propellers were the type of ship best suited to ocean crossings and they were used accordingly. The heavier armoured frigates, on the other hand, plied between home ports. In 1876, for example, all the corvettes and training ships, except *Arcona* and *Albatross,* were out in foreign waters. On average they covered two-thirds of the distance under sail, the other third under steam. Assignments carried out on these voyages were many and varied: scientific forays in the fields of oceanography, ethnography and geography, especially with the purpose of carrying out surveys; training exercises for boy sailors and cadets; safeguarding of German trading interests; and minor political missions, where necessary, intended to advance German economic and diplomatic influence—by "showing the flag". This was the case with, amongst others, the *Vineta* and *Gazelle* in Haiti in 1872, with four corvettes and two gunboats in China, and in the same year with an armoured squadron off Turkey at Saloniki, as well as with the *Elisabeth, Leipzig, Medusa* and *Ariadne* serving off the coast of Central America in 1878.

The flush-decked corvette *Luise,* pictured below, was launched in 1874 from the Imperial Shipyard in Danzig. She was built along the same lines as her sister ship *Ariadne* and differed only in detail from the *Freya.* A carvel-built ship displacing 1692 t, she was 68 m long and ran on a double expansion engine. Full-rigged, she had a sail area of 1582 sqm and could do 14 knots. The crew numbered 13 officers and 220 men. She was equipped with six 15-cm Krupp cannon and two 12-cm Krupp cannon. From 1875 to 1880 she was in East Asia, then for two years in South America, from 1885 to 1888 a training ship, then a station ship in Kiel. In 1897 she was broken up in Hamburg.

The despatch-boat *Hohenzollern,* seen above, was completed in 1876 by the North German Shipbuilding Company in Kiel. She was an iron ship with a displacement of 1707 t, 90 m long. She carried 356 sqm of sail with schooner rig, had a single-expansion engine to drive her paddle-wheels and could reach 16 knots. The crew numbered 9 officers and 136 men and she was armed with two 12.5-cm Krupp cannon. In 1880 she was put into service as the Imperial Yacht. In 1892, after the completion of the new yacht *Hohenzollern* for Wilhelm II, she was renamed *Kaiseradler.* In 1904 she became the property of the German Crown Prince and was finally broken up in Danzig in 1912.

The *Undine,* shown left, belonged to the same class of training ship as *Musquito* and *Rover.* She was launched in 1869 at the Royal Shipyard in Danzig. She displaced 670 t, was 42 m long, was armed with eight 24-pounder cannon and had a crew of 8 officers and 142 men. In 1871 she began service as a training ship for boy sailors, but ran ashore on the north coast of Jutland during a storm in 1884. All hands except one were saved.

The despatch-boat *Zieten* was built in London at the Thames Iron Works in 1876. She was an iron ship, powered by two double-expansion engines and rigged as a schooner with 355 sqm of sail. She had a displacement of 1001 t and a length of 80 m, and on her tests reached a speed of 16.3 knots. She was commissioned as a torpedo trials vessel and at bow and stern had a 38-cm calibre torpedo tube below the waterline. From 1878 to 1888 she was under the command of Tirpitz. It was under his direction that the German torpedo force was built up during this period. In 1899 the *Zieten* was overhauled to serve as a guard ship to the fishing fleet, and the photograph above was taken during this time. In 1919 she was taken out of service and was scrapped in 1921.

On the left is an old photograph of the armoured corvette *Hansa* moored to a buoy in the harbour at Kiel.

On the right is a photograph of the armoured ship *Preussen,* also moored to a buoy in Kiel harbour.

The illustration on the left shows the armoured corvette *Sachsen* during construction at the Vulcan Shipyard at Stettin; on the right is the same ship after her commissioning.

Stosch's plan did not embrace a powerful ocean-going fleet, but instead a home-based fleet consisting of the strongest units, whose essential job was to provide an active defence of the coasts in the case of a war on land. Following this plan, four so-called corvettes of the Sachsen Class were designed and built in the seventies. They were distinguished by their four funnels arranged in a square and by their box-type superstructures. The first to be launched was the *Sachsen,* completed at the Vulcan yards in July 1877. She was followed in May and November respectively by the *Bayern* and *Württemberg* and finally by the *Baden,* in July 1880, all launched at the Imperial Shipyard in Kiel. These iron ships displaced on average 7800 t, were 98 m long and could maintain between 13 and 14 knots. Their twin four-blade screws were driven by two single-expansion engines. The ships had a crew of 32 officers and 285 men. Each had wrought-iron armour-plating and was fitted, at first, with six 26-cm guns, of which two were in armoured casemates amidships and two were in a turret forward. In addition each disposed six 8.7-cm Krupp cannon and eight 3.7-cm revolving cannon, and after 1886 a swivel-mounted stern torpedo tube and two bow torpedo tubes. In the nineties, the ships were rebuilt, so that they retained only one funnel and their quick-firing guns. In 1910 they were taken out of service and were subsequently used as target ships (the *Württemberg* as a training and trials vessel), before being broken up after the First World War. The *Baden* was the last to go; she was broken up in 1939/40.

Right: a photograph of a Sachsen Class ship of the 1880s.

The first design-built gunboats of the Imperial Navy were eleven Wasp-Class boats built in 1875 according to official requirements: *Wespe, Viper, Biene, Mücke, Scorpion, Basilisk, Chamäleon, Crocodill, Salamander, Natter* and *Hummel.* They were all iron-clad ships, commissioned from the Weser Company in Bremen and launched between 1876 and 1881. They displaced 1098 t, were 46 m long, ran on two double-expansion engines, could do 11 knots and were armed with a 30.5-cm Krupp cannon. On the open seas they shipped a lot of water and were hardly usable even in Force 4 winds. But with their flat hulls they could readily be beached on the flats at ebb tide and serve there as stationary batteries. They made scarcely any voyages and were finally taken out of service in 1910. Most of them were scrapped a few years later.

The gunboat *Otter,* launched in 1877 by the Schichau Shipyard in Danzig, was intended expressly for use against pirates on the Chinese coast, who were becoming dangerous to German merchant ships. Yet she never embarked on a foreign voyage. She was a transverse-ribbed iron ship, with two single-expansion engines, 31 m long and having a displacement of 130 t. The crew comprised one officer and 42 men. The *Otter* was used as a mine training ship, was taken out of service in 1907, became a coal barge, and was scrapped in 1926.

In contrast with the armoured boats of the Wasp Class, three smaller, unarmoured gunboats, *Wolf, Hyäne* and *Iltis,* were built later at the Imperial Shipyard in Wilhelmshaven. They were launched together in 1878, displaced 490 t and were 47 m long, could easily do 9 knots and had two 12.5-cm Krupp cannon and two 8.7-cm Krupp cannon each. They were fitted with engines from the Chameleon Class gunboats *Blitz, Basilisk* and *Delphin.* At first they had barquentine rigging, with 847 sqm of sail, and later carried a schooner rig. They were ocean-going ships and often voyaged overseas with their crews of 5 officers and 80 men.

From 1879 to 1884 *Wolf* was in East Asia, then was used as a survey ship, and was in West Africa between 1898 and 1905. After her withdrawal from service, she became a repair ship in Danzig from 1906 until 1919 when she was scrapped. *Hyäne* spent the years from 1879 to 1887 in the Pacific, calling in 1882 amongst other places at Easter Island to carry out research work and, with the frigate *Elisabeth,* hoisting the flag at Matupi on the occasion of the acquisition of the Bismarck Archipelago for the Reich in October 1884. She was in West Africa between 1888 and 1898, then became a survey ship and was stationed during World War I at the mouth of the Eider as a guard ship. She was sold to a private shipping company in 1919, becoming a freighter under the name of *Seewolf,* and was sunk in 1924 off Dieppe after her cargo had caught fire.

After her commissioning in 1880, the *Iltis,* pictured above, served in East Asia. On 23rd July 1896 she ran into a typhoon in the Yellow Sea, was tossed on to the rocks south-east of the Shantung Peninsula, and sank. Of the crew, five officers, including the commanding officer Lieutenant Otto Braun, and 71 men, lost their lives. Only 11 men were rescued.

On the left is a photograph of the Bismarck-Class protected corvette *Gneisenau.*

Service on board was governed by a strict routine, which laid down when the crew were required to get up, eat or perform particular duties to the exact minute. As in the maritime services of other nations, the main features of this traditional routine survived until after the Second World War. A blast on the whistle from the boatswain roused the men at 5.00 am. By 5.05 the hammocks in which the men had slept had to be lashed or tied up with string and stowed away. Between 5.10 and 5.40 was the time for washing and dressing and this was followed by cleaning the ship, a general tidy-up, which was carried out barefoot in summer. Then there was mess duty at 6.50, when the messhands who had been detailed to mess duty for the day set up the tables and benches, which were mostly fastened under the deck, and fetched coffee from the galley. From 7.00 until 7.40 there was a breakfast break, followed by clearing the deck and colors parade at 8.00 on the upper deck. At 8.10 cleaning of the guns began, at 8.45 cleaning of the small-arms, at 9.00 preparation for inspection; and at 9.10 the daily inspection, similar to roll-call in the army, took place. General drill followed between 9.30 and 11.30, at the end of which the "Clear the Decks" signal was blown on the whistle and

the deck was swept and tidied. 11.45 meant mess duty again and at 12.00 the crew were summoned by the call "All Hands to Lunch". The men's meal consisted of meat or saltmeat, either with pulses and potatoes, dried fruit and dumplings, or cooked together with mashed potatoes. The commanding officer, ship's doctor and paymaster were obliged to taste the meal, but generally ate something better themselves. While in port tradesmen selling provisions and other requisites were allowed on board during the midday break, but had to disembark again at 13.45. Between 14.00 and 16.00 there was "Division Duty": instruction, uniform inspection, rifle practice and so on. At 16.00 the "Clear the Decks" signal was sounded again and there was a short break, followed at 16.30 by another hour's duties. Then came a final "Clear the Decks" at the end of the day's duties at 17.30, the last "Mess-room Duty" at 17.50 and at 18.00 the evening meal, which consisted of tea and bread and butter. During the ensuing free period, the potatoes had to be

peeled ready for the next day. The decks were swept again at 20.50, then there was "Pipes and Matches Out" in the lower living quarters, for at night smoking was allowed on deck only, and at 21.00, after the bandsman had beaten or blown the retreat, the whistle for "All Quiet in the Ship" was sounded.

At sea service ran according to the Sea Routine: the colors parade and the rising and retiring signals were omitted because the crew, divided into watches, maintained continuous 24-hour duty, taking turns every four hours. At a time when there were no radios, records or tape recorders, the ship's band filled an important gap in the crew's leisure time. They spent a lot of time singing songs, amongst them the famous sea shanties, sailors' working songs. They also often danced to the music of the band and there were a series of typical leisure games such as "Hot Cockles", of which one may gain some idea from the photograph below, taken on the deck of the corvette *Stosch*.

The drawing on the left, dated 1880, shows sailors during the midday break on a corvette at sea. Below is a photograph, taken at about the same time, of the crew of the *Stosch* watching two of their number at the very popular "Strop Game". The winner was the one who succeeded in pulling the other over the marker-line with the strop behind his neck.

The photograph above shows the corvette *Stosch* during her period of service as a training ship for naval cadets and boy sailors, after 1888.

The artillery on the large wooden ships-of-the-line consisted of long rows of gun emplacements behind cannon ports on battery decks. The only one of these ships which the Prusso-German navy ever owned was the former British *Renown* and she was not used for anything other than training purposes. She had two closed decks and boasted a total of 91 gun ports, but as a German gunnery training ship she never carried her full complement and was always armed in varying degree according to her training function.

Warships with a covered gun deck and, on the upper deck, additional guns which could fire through embrasures in the sides of the quarter-deck, were originally called frigates; after the advent of steam engines, however, they were mostly called "protected corvettes". True corvettes, which were called "flush-decked corvettes" to distinguish them from the protected corvettes, had guns on the upper deck only. Unarmoured protected corvettes and cruising frigates were being built into the eighties with gun emplacements behind ports on a closed battery deck.

Until the middle of the century, the cannon were muzzle-loaders—and they fired round iron cannonballs, according to whose weight in pounds the guns were classified. The first armoured frigates of the 1860s were still fitted with ports for 72-pounders, but were later given modern Krupp guns, breech-loaders with rifled 24- and 21-cm bores. They were built-up cannon—around the barrel were a variable number of hoops of different thicknesses, according to the distance of the part of the barrel from the chamber. Only the bores themselves were cast in one piece out of cast steel. The old muzzle-loading cannon, on the other hand, consisted of a cast-iron or bronze bore closed at the back.

The armoured ships of the seventies had a large casemate, a gun room with armoured walls usually protruding from the side of the ship. The installation of guns in armoured revolving turrets, which later became universal, was seen first in 1865 on an English-built ship, the *Arminius*. In 1873 the armoured frigate *Preussen* became the first German-built ship to be equipped in this way. Instead of round iron cannonballs, bullet-shaped projectiles were used in the rifled breech-loaders. These shells were many times heavier than the old cannonballs and tapered to a point.

Below is a view of the battery deck of a cruising frigate during gun practice around 1880. In front on the left is a cartridge, and standing next to it a shell in a portable frame can be seen.

The English Armstrong cannon illustrated right was installed in 1865 in a domed turret on the *Arminius*. This was a 21-cm calibre gun, four metres long. On the right in front of it is a shell; the hoops on this built-up cannon can be clearly seen.

The illustration on the left shows the firing of a 26-cm Krupp cannon in the turret of an armoured corvette of the Sachsen Class.

The gunnery training ship *Mars*, shown on the right, was built according to specifications drawn up by the authorities in 1876. She was launched in 1879 at the Imperial Shipyard in Wilhelmshaven, displaced 3251 t, was 84 m long and could do a bare 12 knots. According to the demands of training service, she was variously equipped and crewed. She was not taken out of service until 1914, when she served as living quarters before being scrapped.

The illustration above shows sailors at gun practice on board the despatch-boat *Habicht,* which, together with *Möwe* and *Adler,* belonged to a class of gunboats launched between 1879 and 1883. They displaced about 860 t, were 60 m long and logged a speed of 11.5 knots. Until 1905/06 they were stationed exclusively abroad and then became training ships until the end of their days in service—with the exception of the *Adler,* which ran ashore at Samoa in a hurricane in 1889. The ships were armed with one 15-cm and four 12-cm Krupp cannon each. One of these can be seen in the picture.

Side by side with the artillery, small-arms played a considerable role during the 19th century, not only as infantry weapons used in land engagements but also in battles fought at close range at sea. The picture above shows marksmen at the top of a cruising frigate, firing rifles and machine-guns during a manoeuvre.

The last Bismarck-Class cruising frigate to be put in service was the *Stein,* launched in September 1879 by AG. Vulcan in Stettin. She served overseas until 1888 and then as a training ship for cadets and cabin-boys until 1908. The photograph on the right was taken during this latter period.

In 1885 the last full-rigged armed warship of the German Navy was launched at the Imperial Shipyard in Wilhelmshaven. This was the cruising frigate *Charlotte*, 84 m long, displacing almost 3300 t and similar to the ships of the Bismarck Class. She too began service abroad and afterwards, from 1897 to 1909, was a training ship. She was subsequently taken out of service. A photograph of her is reproduced overleaf.

On page 81 is a reproduction of a famous painting by Hans Petersen of the cruising frigate *Gneisenau* under studding-sail. At the World Exhibition in Paris in 1900 this painting was awarded first prize. It now hangs in the Naval College at Mürwik.

On the right is pictured one of the Siegfried Class of ships.

The ship in the photograph on the left is the *Olga*, launched in 1880 by AG. Vulcan in Stettin. She is seen here after her reconstruction in 1892, without rigging.

Left: The despatch-boat *Blitz*, launched in 1882 by the North German Shipbuilding Company in Kiel, after being rebuilt in the 1890s. The rigging on this, as on most of the rigged ships built in the 1880s, was removed before the turn of the century.

In the eighties a series of other rigged ships besides the *Charlotte* were built, most of them intended to serve as cruisers in foreign waters. These were: the flush-decked corvettes *Carola*, *Olga*, *Marie*, *Sophie*, *Alexandrine* and *Arcona*, all launched between 1880 and 1885, barque-rigged with 1 200 sqm of sail, displacing either 2 147 or 2 361 t and 76 or 81 m long; the despatch-boats *Blitz* and *Pfeil*, square-rigged schooners of 1 486 t and 78 m in length, launched in 1882; the flush-decked corvette *Nixe*, having a sail area of 1 580 sqm fully-rigged, weighing 1 781 t and measuring 63 m long, launched at Danzig's Imperial Shipyard in July 1885; and finally the cruisers *Schwalbe* and *Sperber*, rigged fore-and-aft as barques, with a displacement of 1 111 t and a length of 70 m, and launched at the Imperial Shipyard in Wilhelmshaven. These were followed in rapid succession in the years between 1888 and 1895 by the cruisers *Bussard*, *Falke*, *Seeadler*, *Condor*, *Cor-*

moran and *Geier*. They were each about 1 600 t and around 83 m long and were armed with gun-turrets fore and aft. With the exception of later unarmed sailing ships intended for instruction purposes only and of the gunboat *Meteor* built in 1915, with its barque tackle, these cruisers were the very last warships in the German navy built to take rigging.

It is also interesting to note that the eighties were distinguished by the colonial policy of the Reich, in which the Navy's foreign cruisers actively participated. When treaties were being signed with indigenous rulers upon the creation of German protectorates or when the flag was hoisted in newly-acquired territories, German warships were mostly present on the scene.

In 1883 Lieutenant-General von Caprivi took over from Admiral von Stosch as Chief of the Admiralty. Upon taking up his post, he drew attention to the need for armoured battleships, a "combat-ready

ocean-going fleet". Nevertheless the tempo of ship construction slowed down under his direction—and in the last analysis, his approach to the creation of a fleet was, like that of his predecessor, influenced by European continental considerations.

There now came into being the first new, large vessels designed from the start not to have any sailing tackle. At the AG. Vulcan yard in Stettin the steel armoured ship *Oldenburg* was launched in 1884. She was a casemated ship with eight 24-cm and two 8.7-cm Krupp cannon, and had 34 officers and 355 men. Displacing 5 249 t and 80 m long, she had two double-expansion engines driving twin 3-blade screws, giving a top speed of 14 knots. After serving in the home fleet and abroad in the Levant, the *Oldenburg* became a guard ship in 1900. From 1912, after being taken out of service, she was used as a target ship, before being broken up in 1919.

Both the cruising corvettes *Irene* and

Prinzess Wilhelm, though begun only a few years later, also carried no sail. They were steel ships 104 m long, displacing 4271 t and logging 18 knots with two double-expansion engines and twin screws. *Irene* was launched in 1887 by AG. Vulcan in Stettin, her sister ship in the Germania Shipyard in Kiel in the same year. Both ships were equipped with 14 15-cm Krupp cannon. They voyaged abroad until 1900, were taken out of service in 1914 and were scrapped after the War, in 1921 and 1922 respectively.

Apart from new despatch-boats (*Greif* 1886, Guard Class 1887) and larger gunboats (*Brummer* Class 1884, *Eber* 1887) which were all-steel ships, and of which the only one with sails was the *Eber,* lost in a hurricane in Apia harbour in 1889, the most important new constructions designed under Caprivi's direction were the *Siegfried* Class of armoured coastal vessels. All of them—*Siegfried* (launched 1889), *Beowulf* (1890), *Frithjof* (1892) and *Hagen,*

as well as the similar *Odin* (1894) and *Ägir* (1895) designed in 1892—were used to protect the coast in World War I. They were steel ships, displacing about 3500 t and measuring 79 m long, driven by two triple-expansion engines and twin screws at a speed of around 15 knots, and having a crew of 20 officers and 256 men. Three 21-cm guns, each in a turret, were on the port bow, on the starboard bow and astern midships. In addition there were four 8.8-cm quick-firing cannon on both sides. The complete group of ships was rebuilt shortly after 1900, each vessel receiving two funnels in place of the original one. From 1890 to 1897 they carried torpedo nets. They were not laid up until after the First World War, when some of them were scrapped and others sold to private shipping companies for use as freighters. *Odin* survived longest, until 1935.

In 1887 Wilhelm I had laid the foundations of the canal which later bore his name,

the Kaiser Wilhelm (or Kiel) Canal. The canal was intended to make ships travelling between the North Sea and the Baltic independent of the only other route then possible, which led through the Sound and the Belts, outside German territorial waters. When the Kaiser died a year later, followed by his son Friedrich III only a few months afterwards, the establishment of the naval services which passed on Wilhelm II's succession to the throne numbered 15,480, including 534 naval officers. The fleet comprised 13 armoured ships of varying age, 8 cruising frigates employed overseas and for training, 10 cruising corvettes, of which *Irene* and *Prinzess Wilhelm* were the only two to have twin screws and no sailing tackle, 14 small armoured coastal vessels, 5 cruisers, 5 gunboats, 6 despatch-boats, 10 training ships and 9 additional small vessels which served a whole range of different purposes. This, then, was the fleet inherited by Kaiser Wilhelm II.

Below: a printed pocket handkerchief of 1895, showing the most important new types of ships in service or in construction at the time of Wilhelm II's succession. Only the Brandenburg-Class armoured ship *Kurfürst Friedrich Wilhelm* and the Kaiser's yacht, the new *Hohenzollern,* were planned and commissioned after this date. The round panel in the centre shows the Kaiser on the left, on the right his brother Prince Heinrich, who had been a naval officer since 1877 and who was promoted to Rear-Admiral in 1895, and behind them the Kaiser's son, Prince Adalbert, who entered the navy in 1894 as a sub-lieutenant.

The Imperial Navy under Wilhelm II 1888–1918

Wilhelm II brought with him to the throne a deep personal interest in navigation and naval matters. As a boy, he had sailed, and had even sketched a few designs for warships. He was greatly impressed by the theories of the American naval historian A.T. Mahan and it was a momentous day for the navy when this sea-loving monarch became its supreme commander. (By way of contrast, Germany's peace-time army was largely under the control of the princes). Caprivi, who had followed Bismarck as

Chancellor in 1890, already had been replaced by Vice-Admiral Graf Monts in July 1888. The latter was the first Chief of the Admiralty who had actually served as a naval officer. Unfortunately, he died within six months and had to be replaced by Vice-Admiral Baron von der Goltz.

In 1892, the royal yacht *Hohenzollern* was launched from the AG. Vulcan yards in Stettin. Designed in 1890 as a despatch-boat, she had a displacement of 4180 t and was 122 m long. Her two triple-expansion

engines gave her a speed of 21.5 knots. The Kaiser, an enthusiastic sailor, made most of his journeys abroad in this ship. The *Hohenzollern* was taken out of service when war broke out and in 1923 was broken up for scrap. The above picture shows the 1895 dedication of the North Sea-Baltic Canal. The Kaiser, whose standard flies from the mainmast, receives honors on the signal bridge from the assembled fleet in Kiel Harbour.

The naval cabinet was formed in the spring of 1889, with responsibility for the administration and staffing of the officer corps. At its head was a flag-officer of the Kaiser's retinue, the first being Captain von Senden-Bibran. At the same time, the navy's command structure was changed. The Admiralty was replaced by the Naval High Command, led by Vice-Admiral von der Goltz, and the Imperial Navy Office, under the Secretary of State for the Navy. This latter authority also included the all-important construction section, responsible for the design and building of the navy's ships.

The first Secretary of State for the Navy was Rear-Admiral von Heusner, followed in 1897 by Rear-Admiral Tirpitz. Commander of the torpedo-boat *Zieten* in 1877, later in the administrative office of the tor-pedo branch and, after his appointment in 1886, its chief inspector, Tirpitz made many important contributions to the design of the torpedo and its tactical use as a modern weapon of war.

A torpedo division had been formed in Wilhelmshaven as early as 1871 under Commander Graf von Monts (later Chief of the Admiralty). Von Monts had been present when the Austrian inventor, Luppis, demonstrated the first torpedo in Fiume in 1869. He approached the Englishman, Whitehead, who had taken over the patent rights, and arranged for the new weapon to be manufactured by the Berlin firm of Schwartzkopf under licence in 1873. In the same year, the gunboat *Basilisk* had her 15.5-cm cannon replaced by a torpedo tube, becoming the first torpedo-boat of the Imperial Navy. Previously, the term "torpedo" had been applied to any explosive charge operating under water; the two earlier series of so-called "torpedo-boats" were in fact small steamers, launched in 1871 from the yards of Devrient in Danzig and Waltjen & Co. in Bremen, carrying an explosive-tipped ram at the bow. The first three, known as the "Devrient Boats", were rebuilt in 1881 and, carrying a "torpedo-launching-tube" in the bows, became Germany's first true torpedo-boats. They were steel-built, 20 m long and displaced 34 t. Their single-expansion engines gave them a speed of eight knots. They were named simply *I*, *II* and *III*. Other ram-type torpedo-boats were the *Notus*, *Zephir* and *Rival* (AG. Vulcan, Stettin, 1872—74) and the 37-m, twin-funnelled steamer *Ulan* (Möller

& Hollberg, Stettin, 1876) which was later fitted with a torpedo tube and designated *IV*.

The next series of boats, *V* to *XI* (AG. Weser, Bremen, 1882) were also given names; the first, *Schütze,* giving her name to the class. During 1884/85, various yards competed in the design of new torpedo-boats. These were identified by the initial letter of the yard followed by a serial-number: *W1* to *W6* (AG. Weser, Bremen); *V1* to *V10* (AG. Vulcan, Stettin); *S1* to *S6* (F. Schichau, Elbing); *Th1* and *Th2* (John J. Thorneycroft & Co., Chiswick); *Y* (Yarrow & Co., London) and *G* (Germania yards, Kiel). As the Schichau design proved itself superior to those of competing yards, the rest of the boats built between 1885 and 1898, the *S7* to *S87,* were built at Elbing. Opposite: A torpedo-boat of the early eighties lying in dock. Above: One of the *S7–S57* series of torpedo-boats breaks through a formation led by the battleship *Brandenburg.*

Tactically, the torpedo-boat was designed for a high-speed approach to within the optimal firing-range of her torpedoes, at that time a mere 200 metres. Over the years, these little boats became bigger and faster: the *S7* (1885) displaced 86 t, was 38 m long and could make 20 knots; the *S87* (1897) was 142 t, 48 m, and could make 25.3 knots. They were usually armed with two deck-mounted torpedo tubes and one below the waterline in the bows. In addition, they had two 3.7-cm revolving-barrel cannon, later replaced by a 5-cm quick-firing gun on the torpedo mount. They had one officer and 15 crew. Six boats formed a division, led by a torpedo division-boat. These boats, distinguished by the letter "D" and a serial number, were also built in Schichau. The *D1* (249 t, 56 m) was launched in 1886, the *D9* (350 t, 63 m) in 1894. The last boat in this series, the *D10,* was built by Thorneycroft in 1898. They made between 20 and 24 knots and were armed similarly to the smaller boats except that they had six 3.7-cm revolver guns, later replaced by three 5-cm quick-firing-guns.

The Schichau torpedo-boats were then the fastest craft in the world and twice broke the world speed record over water: in 1888 with 28.4 knots and in 1897 with 36.7. As a result, they were used in the days before the advent of radio as both despatch-boats and signal relays.

Left: The *Wörth* and *Weissenburg* under full steam fire their main batteries during fleet manoeuvres. In the foreground, a torpedo-boat of the series *S67—S73* relays signals. (From a watercolour by Willy Stöwer.)

Above: The battleship *Kaiser Friedrich III* from a painting by H. Graf.

In 1891, three ships of a new class were launched. They were large, armoured vessels mounting three heavy gun turrets, and were the first modern ships to receive the old title of "ships-of-the-line". They were the *Kurfürst Friedrich Wilhelm* (Imperial Shipyard, Wilhelmshaven), *Brandenburg* and *Weissenburg* (AG. Vulcan, Stettin). They were followed by the *Wörth* (Germania yards, Kiel) in 1892. These Brandenburg-Class ships had displacements of 10,013 t, were 116 m long and their two triple-expansion engines driving twin 5-m

diameter screws gave them speeds of between 16 and 17 knots. They were armed with six 28-cm guns, six rapid-loading cannon of 10.5 cm and eight of 8.8 cm calibre, and six torpedo tubes. They had a complement of 38 officers and 530 men. They were sent, as Division 1 of the First Battleship Squadron, to reinforce the international forces in China during the Boxer Uprising. In 1910, the *Kurfürst Friedrich Wilhelm* and the *Weissenburg* were sold to the Turkish navy. The former, sailing under the name *Heireddin Barbarossa*, was sunk by torpedoes from a British submarine in the Dardanelles in 1915. In 1915, the *Brandenburg* and *Wörth* were used as coast defence ships; in 1919 they were retired from service and broken up in Danzig.

In 1896, the first of another series of battleships was launched at the Imperial Shipyard in Wilhelmshaven. This was the *Kaiser Friedrich III,* which gave her name to the so-called "New Kaiser Class" (a name which reverted in 1911 to "Old Kaiser Class" with the building of yet another series, and which also became known as the "Kaiser Friedrich Class"). She was followed by the *Kaiser Wilhelm II* (Imperial Shipyard, 1896), the *Kaiser Wilhelm der Grosse* (Germania yards, Kiel, 1899), *Kaiser Karl der Grosse* (Blohm & Voss, Hamburg, 1899) and the *Kaiser Barbarossa* (Schichau, Danzig, 1900), all built to plans prepared by the Navy Office. They were 125 m long, displaced 11,097 t and their three triple-expansion engines drove them at speeds up to 18 knots. Their armament consisted of four 24-cm, eighteen 15-cm and twelve 8.8-cm rapid-loading cannon, twelve 3.7-cm heavy machine-guns and six torpedo tubes. After service with the fleet they were used as station ships. They were retired in 1919 and scrapped.

Left: The battleship *Kaiser Friedrich III* at her berth.

Right: Brandenburg-Class ships in line astern during manoeuvres, their guns trained to starboard. In the foreground, the *Brandenburg* herself.

Overleaf: (Above) the *Brandenburg* under full steam. (Below) her sister ship, the *Kurfürst Friedrich Wilhelm,* both from paintings by H. Graf dated 1899.

The illustrations on the previous page, taken from paintings by H. Graf, show (top) the launching of the large cruiser *Vineta* in 1897 and (bottom) the *König Wilhelm*, once an armoured frigate but converted to a large cruiser in 1897.

From the end of the eighties onwards, the cruising frigates, now entirely without sails, were renamed "large cruisers". The corvettes became "light cruisers". 1892 saw the launching of the *Kaiserin Augusta* from the Germania docks in Kiel—a large cruiser displacing 6056 t and 123 m at the waterline. She was the Navy's first triple-screw ship and, with her three triple-expansion engines, she boasted a speed of just under 21.6 knots. With a complement of 13 officers and 417 men, her armament consisted of four 15-cm guns, eight 8.8-cm quick firing cannon, four revolving cannon and five torpedo tubes. She saw service in North America, Morocco and the Mediterranean. From 1914 until 1920, when she was finally broken up, she served as an artillery training ship. Her three funnels set the pattern for subsequent large cruisers of the Viktoria Luise Class: the *Viktoria Luise*, the *Hertha*, the *Freya* (all of 5660 t) and the *Vineta* and *Hansa* (5885 t). These ships, built at various yards and launched in 1897 and 1899, were all 110 m long and were capable of around 19 knots. Each carried two 21-cm, eight 15-cm and ten 8.8-cm quick firing cannon, ten heavy machineguns and three torpedo tubes. Crews consisted of 31 officers and 446 men. (See page 102). In 1897 the armoured cruiser *Fürst Bismarck* ran down the slips at the Imperial Shipyard at Kiel. With a length of 127 m, she displaced 10,690 t. Her armament comprised four 24-cm, twelve 15-cm and ten 8.8-cm rapid-loading cannon, and three torpedo tubes. She had two funnels and, with three triple-expansion engines, could make 18.7 knots. Between 1900 and 1908 she served with Germany's East Asian Squadron, was used as a target ship during World War I, and was broken up in 1920.

Triple-expansion marine engines were also used in the light cruisers of the 1890s, giving them speeds of a good 20 knots. These ships included the three-funnelled *Gefion* (Schichau, 1893), the single-funnelled *Hela* (AG. Weser, 1895) and the twin-funnelled Gazelle-Class ships built at various yards between 1898 and 1902. In this class were the *Gazelle, Niobe, Nymphe, Thetis, Ariadne, Amazone, Medusa, Frauenlob, Arcona* and *Undine* (see pp. 103—4). The *Gefion* displaced 3746 t and was 110 m in length; the *Hela*, 2027 t, 105 m. Ships in the Gazelle Class were also 105 m long but had a displacement of 2700 t. Except for the *Hela*, which carried four 8.8-cm and six 5-cm quick firing cannon, all these ships were armed with ten 10.5-cm quick firing cannon and three torpedo tubes.

The armoured frigates *König Wilhelm, Kaiser* and *Deutschland* were all rebuilt during the nineties; sails disappeared and up-to-date armament was installed.

The engraving opposite shows mess-hands fetching rations from the galley of an old armoured frigate.

Above, the *Kaiser*, once an armoured frigate, shown here after her 1891–95 rebuild as a large cruiser.

The older armoured ships of the Sachsen Class, with their two pairs of funnels, were also rebuilt during the mid-nineties. Their engines and boilers were modernised, quick firing armament was installed and a single funnel replaced the original four.

The illustrations on the opposite page show (top) the *Sachsen* after her rebuild, (centre) the Viktoria-Luise-Class heavy cruiser *Hertha* and (bottom) the Iltis-Class gunboat *Jaguar*.

The *Iltis* and the *Jaguar* were launched in 1898 at Schichau. Other ships in this class were the *Tiger*, *Luchs* and *Panther*, built from 1899 to 1901 at the Imperial Shipyard in Danzig, and the *Eber* at Stettiner Vulcan in 1903. They displaced between 894 and 977 t, were around 66 m long and made 14 knots. The *Iltis* and the *Jaguar* were armed with four 8.8-cm quick firing cannon while the others had only two, of 10.5-cm calibre. They had a complement of nine officers and 121 men. All saw service in foreign waters; except for the *Panther* (see page 109) and the *Eber* they took part in the relief of Tsingtao and were there when, in November 1914, the city fell to the Japanese. Rather than permit their capture by the enemy, the ships were scuttled. The *Eber*, too, fared badly. In 1914, having joined up with the auxiliary cruiser *Cap Trafalgar* off Trinidad, she was interned in Brazil and, in 1917, in Bahia, sunk by her crew. In 1900, during the Boxer Rebellion, the *Iltis* played a decisive role in the capture of the Chinese forts at Taku. For this she became the only German naval vessel to receive the French Order of Merit.

In 1892 the Kaiser appointed Tirpitz Chief of Staff of the Naval High Command. In 1897 he succeeded Heusner as Secretary of State for the Navy. During the following year, already nominated as a Minister of State, he became the driving force behind legislation for the rebuilding of German naval power—legislation which was finally passed by the Reichstag in 1898. It laid down the number of ships needed for the navy and required their replacement after a fixed service life of 25 years for battleships, 20 years for large cruisers and 15 years for light cruisers. By the end of 1903 Germany's naval strength (including reserve units) was to be 19 battleships, eight armoured coastal vessels, 12 large cruisers and 30 light cruisers. The battleships were to consist of four armoured ships of the Sachsen Class; the *Oldenburg;* four Brandenburg-Class vessels; five ships of the new Kaiser Class then being built, and five of the projected Wittelsbach Class. The eight armoured coastal ships were to be Siegfried Class while the *König Wilhelm, Kaiser, Deutschland, Kaiserin Augusta,* five Viktoria-Luise-Class ships, the *Fürst Bismarck* and the planned *Prinz Heinrich* and *Prinz Adalbert* were heavy cruisers.

Pictured below: Sailors aboard a cruiser on parade with their rolled-up hammocks.

By the end of the century, the Navy had (according to official records for the fiscal year ending 1899) a combined strength of 28,764 men. Of these, 11,887 were sailors, 6569 engine-room personnel, 2690 torpedo hands, 2198 naval gunners, 1239 marines, 358 medical corpsmen and a few hundred in various other posts. There was also a total of 1733 administrative officials amongst whom was the only woman—a teacher. Of the 1118 officers, 852 were line officers, 128 were engineers and 40 were with the marines. The gunnery branch had 57 officers and there were 26 torpedo officers and 15 mine officers. The medical branch had 142 medical officers. In addition, there were 1119 warrant officers and 5193 petty officers, leaving a total of 18,159 ratings and 1300 naval cadets.

Admirals and vice-admirals received an annual salary of 12,000 goldmarks, captains on active service, 7800, lieutenants, 3900, and sub-lieutenants, 900. By way of further example, warrant officers received 1692 goldmarks, petty-officers 540, able seamen 288, and naval cadets 144. The officer in command of the German Navy, Tirpitz, had an annual salary of 30,000 goldmarks and a free residence.

The outbreak of the Boer War and other political incidents, such as the Samoan dispute and tension between the Spanish-American States, gave Tirpitz the opportunity to push a second Bill through the Reichstag in 1900, doubling the required number of battleships and raising the rest of the projected fleet to 14 large cruisers, 38 light cruisers and 96 torpedo-boats. New Acts of 1906, 1908 and 1912 raised the numbers even further. Requirements for the end of 1917 stood at 41 battleships, 20 heavy (battle) cruisers and 40 light cruisers. The planned service life of heavy ships was reduced to 20 years.

Two battleships of the Kaiser Friedrich
Class: left, the *Kaiser Barbarossa;* above, the
Kaiser Wilhelm II.

Above, the off-duty watch of the battleship *Kaiser Wilhelm II* relaxes on the forecastle. Left, a photograph of a sister ship, *Kaiser Wilhelm der Grosse,* at her moorings in Kiel Harbour.

In 1895, Admiral von Knorr had relieved Goltz of his position as Chief of the Naval High Command. In 1899 the Kaiser declared himself Supreme Commander and, instead of the High Command, established an Admiralty which was to last until the end of World War I. The first Chief of Staff was Rear-Admiral Bendemann, followed soon after by Vice-Admiral von Diederichs. The Admiralty, Naval Office and the Naval Ministry became independent bodies responsible directly to the Kaiser. In 1900 the heavy fighting ships were brought under the command of the first Admiral of the Fleet, Admiral von Koester. Under him they received their battle training—long and arduous hours of exercises and manoeuvres. Admiral Prinz Heinrich took over from Koester in 1906 and was followed in 1909 by Admiral von Holtzendorff and, from 1912 until 1915, Admiral von Ingenohl.

The photograph below shows a view over the stern of a battleship of the Kaiser Friedrich Class. In the foreground, the rear gun turret with its two 24-cm guns.

The large cruiser *Viktoria Luise*, built 1896/98 at the AG. Weser yards in Bremen. After foreign service she became a training ship from 1908 to 1912, a mine-layer from 1915 to 1918 and, stripped of her guns in 1920, ended her days as a freighter. She was broken up in 1923.

The large cruiser *Freya*, built 1896/98 at the Imperial Shipyard, Danzig after her rebuild in 1913, her original three funnels reduced to two.

The large cruiser *Hansa*, built 1896/98 at the Vulcan yards in Stettin. She was rebuilt in 1909 and, like the *Freya*, lost a funnel in the process.

The light cruiser *Gazelle*, built 1897/1900 at the Germania yards in Kiel. After serving with the fleet and on foreign tours of duty she was a coast defence vessel, then a mine hulk, and was scrapped in 1920.

The light cruiser *Nymphe*, built 1898/1900 at the Germania yards, served with the fleet and as a training ship. Between 1914 and 1916 she sailed on coast defence before being taken over as barracks ship in Kiel. In 1931 she was sold to the breakers for 61,500 reichsmark.

The light cruiser *Amazone*, built 1899/1901 at the Germania yards. She served with the fleet until 1914, as coast defence vessel until 1917, was used then as barracks ship. In 1923, she returned to active service with the fleet. In 1931, became a barracks hulk, eventually for refugees in Bremen, and was finally broken up in 1954 in Hamburg.

The light cruiser *Arcona*, built 1901/03 at AG. Weser in Bremen. She served with the fleet until 1924, was used as barracks ship between 1930 and 1942 and as a floating anti-aircraft battery until May 1945, when she was scuttled in Wilhelmshaven. In 1949, she was raised and broken up.

The light cruiser *Undine*, built 1901/04 at the Howaldts works in Kiel, served as a gunnery training ship. From 1914 she was used for coast defence work, and in November of the following year was hit by torpedoes from the British submarine *E19* and sank off the Danish island of Möen.

The armoured cruiser *Prinz Heinrich* (left and on facing page) was launched at the Imperial Shipyard, Kiel, in 1900. She displaced 8 887 t, was 126.5 m long, and had a top speed of 20.4 knots. Her armaments were two 24-cm, ten 15-cm, and ten 8.8-cm quickfiring cannon and four torpedo tubes. After service with the fleet she was used for administrative offices in Kiel from 1916 until 1920, when she was broken up.

Left: The armoured cruiser *Prinz Adalbert*, launched at the Imperial Shipyard in Kiel in 1901. Except for her three funnels, she was practically a copy of the *Prinz Heinrich*. From 1904 to 1914 she was a gunnery training ship, being sunk by torpedoes from the British submarine *E8* in 1915. Her sister ship, the *Friedrich Carl* (1901/03, Blohm & Voss), was sunk by mines in 1914.

Left: Battleship, the Wittelsbach-Class *Wettin*, launched 1900 at Schichau in Danzig. After service with the fleet became a gunnery training ship. In 1916 she was a barracks ship and was broken up in 1922.

Left: Battleship *Zähringen*, of the Wittelsbach Class. She was built at the Germania yards and launched in 1901. After service with the fleet she was used for naval exercises at Kiel from 1916 onwards. For a while she was left as a hulk but after a rebuild in 1927 was used as a towed target-vessel. In December 1944 she was lost to aerial bombardment off Gdynia.

Right: A Wittelsbach-Class ship on manoeuvres.

Below: To the left, a battleship of the Wittelsbach Class; to the right, a Kaiser-Friedrich-Class vessel.

Opposite: The Iltis-Class gunboat *Panther* which served until 1914 off South America, West Africa and Morocco. She was on coast defence in the Baltic between 1914 and 1918 and, from 1921 to 1926, was engaged in marine survey work. She was scrapped in 1931.

Just as the fighting-power of the Kaiser-Class ships had been increased, so plans were made to improve the Wittelsbach-Class vessels due to be rebuilt between 1899 and 1904.

Tirpitz emphasised the strategy behind the build-up of the fleet: the main objective was a naval force capable of fighting hard, defensive sea battles on the North Sea. But the British were not slow to respond and soon both German and British navies were launched on a spectacular arms race which culminated in the Battle of Jutland—a battle which Tirpitz had foreseen and largely planned for but which was, in the event, strategically futile.

The *Wittelsbach*, launched at the Imperial Shipyard in 1900, the *Wettin* (see page 106), the *Zähringen* (see page 106), the *Schwaben*, also built at the Imperial Shipyard in Wilhelmshaven and launched in 1901, and the *Mecklenburg*, launched at the Vulcan yards in Stettin in 1901, were the five ships of the Wittelsbach Class. They had a displacement of 11,774 t and were 127 m long at the waterline. Their three triple-expansion engines gave them speeds of 17 to 18 knots. Their armament was the same as that of ships of the Kaiser Friedrich Class. They carried a complement of 33 officers and 650 ratings. In 1916, after service with the fleet, all ships were used either as training vessels or barracks ships. Except for the *Zähringen*, which survived until 1944, they were withdrawn from service, broken up during the years 1921/22.

The next series of ships-of-the-line was the Braunschweig Class, built between 1901 and 1906. These were the *Braunschweig* (see page 112), the *Elsass* (see page 112), the *Hessen* (launched at Germania yards, Kiel, in 1903), the *Preussen* (Germania, 1903), and the *Lothringen* (launched 1904 at Schichau in Danzig). They all served with the fleet until 1916, were later taken over by the Merchant Navy and all but one were broken up during the thirties. The exception was the *Hessen*. She took part in the battle of Jutland, in Rear-Admiral Mauve's pre-dreadnought squadron, was used as a radio controlled target vessel during World War II and, in 1946, was handed over to the Soviet Union. Ships of the Braunschweig Class had three funnels; they were 127.7 m long and displaced 13,208 t. They were fitted with three triple-expansion engines and could steam at 18.7 knots. Crews comprised

35 officers and 708 men. They were equipped with four 28-cm, fourteen 17-cm, and eighteen 8.8-cm quickfiring cannon and six torpedo tubes. Stripped of their guns after 1916, the ships were variously armed in the postwar navy.

The *Braunschweig* and her sister ships were the first to be armed with the new rapid-loading, 28-cm calibre guns. Mounted in the fore and aft gun turrets, these were then the heaviest weapons the navy possessed and were subsequently mounted on all battleships and battle-cruisers. They were later replaced by 30.5-cm guns on battleships of the Helgoland Class in 1911 and with 38-cm weapons on the battleship *Bayern* in 1916.

The first modern quickfiring guns with recoiling barrels were of 8.8-cm calibre and were mounted on ships of the Siegfried Class in 1890. In 1892 the *Kaiserin Augusta*

followed with 10.5-cm, and in 1898 the *Viktoria Luise* with 15-cm and 21-cm, and the *Kaiser Friedrich III* with 24-cm rapid-firing guns. Compared with the 4.5-km range of the armoured frigate *König Wilhelm's* 24-cm guns in 1869, by 1898 the 24-cm quickfiring guns aboard Kaiser-Friedrich-Class ships gave them a range of 16.9 km. The firing-rate of these new guns was something like six rounds a minute as against the one round every two or three minutes fired by the older weapons. The shells themselves were correspondingly improved. They were now cylindrical, with a conical tip, and there were three types: exploding shells, their steel jackets filled with explosive and with an impact-detonator in the tip; shrapnel shells which contained ball-shot packed around an explosive charge, and massive armour-piercing shells of solid steel.

On the opposite page are shown the ships of the Braunschweig Class sailing in line a-stern during squadron manoeuvres. Above, the foredeck of the *Preussen* as she cruises in a heavy sea. In the foreground, the two 28-cm guns of her forward turret.

Up to this time, the main batteries of battle-ships had always consisted of pairs of heavy-calibre guns mounted in turrets fore and aft, but their main fighting power amidships lay in the 15-cm or 17-cm guns mounted usually in casemates.

Left: Battleship *Hessen*, launched in 1903 from the Germania yards in Kiel.

Left: Battleship *Elsass*, of the Braunschweig Class, launched 1903 by Schichau in Danzig.

Left: The armoured cruiser *Roon*, launched 1903 from the Imperial Shipyard in Kiel. She was somewhat heavier, longer and faster than her predecessor the *Prinz Adalbert*, and had one more funnel, but was otherwise similarly equipped. After service with the fleet she was used as living quarters in Kiel from 1916 until 1921, when she was broken up.

Right: The armoured cruiser *York,* sister ship of the *Roon,* launched 1904 at Blohm & Voss in Hamburg. She served with the fleet until, in November 1914, she ran into two German mines in the mouth of the Jade and capsized with a loss of 336 men.

Right: The light cruiser *Hamburg* of the Bremen Class, launched 1903 at Vulcan, Stettin. She was with the fleet until 1912 then became flagship for the submarine flotilla. She was used as a training ship during 1926/27, stripped for living quarters in 1936, sunk during aerial bombardment of Hamburg in 1944 and was raised and finally broken up in 1956.

Right: The light cruiser *Lübeck* of the Bremen class, launched 1904 at Vulcan, Stettin. She served with the fleet and, from 1914, on coast defence. From 1917 she was used as a target ship, was handed over to Great Britain in 1920 and broken up in 1922/23.

Left: The Bremen-Class light cruiser *München*, launched 1904 at AG. Weser in Bremen. She was used for torpedo trials, served with the fleet during 1914/15, was then used as a barracks ship and was handed over to Great Britain in 1920.

Left: The Bremen-Class light cruiser *Leipzig*, launched 1905 at AG. Weser, Bremen. She was on foreign service until October 1914 when, forcing her way through the Baltic, she joined Graf Spee's cruiser squadron. She was with the squadron in December of that year when she was sunk by gunfire from the British cruisers *Cornwall* and *Glasgow* off the Falklands, with a loss of 315 men.

Left: The Bremen-Class light cruiser *Danzig*, launched 1905 at the Imperial Shipyard, Danzig. She served with the fleet until 1917, was surrendered to Great Britain in 1920 and was broken up in 1921/23.

Above: (Left to right) the light cruisers *Bremen* and *Berlin* and the armoured cruiser *Roon* in Bergen harbour, Norway. This, and illustrations on the preceding pages, shows the remarkable similarity of the seven Bremen-Class cruisers, which differed only in minor details. The *Bremen* (AG. Weser, 1903) was on foreign service in North America until the outbreak of war, when she joined the fleet and was sunk by mines in December 1915 off Windau in the Baltic. The *Berlin* (Imperial Shipyard, Danzig, 1903) served with the fleet and on foreign duty and, in 1917, on coast defence. During 1923/29 she sailed as a training ship, was converted to living quarters in 1936 and in 1947, loaded with poison-gas canisters from World War II, was sunk in the Skagerrak.

The ships of the Bremen Class were larger than Gazelle-Class vessels and had three funnels. They displaced 3278 t, were 111 m long at the waterline and could make 23 knots. They were armed with ten 10.5-cm quickfiring cannon and two torpedo tubes. All these ships were originally powered by two triple-expansion marine engines but the *Lübeck* was the first ship in the Navy to be equipped with steam-turbines, twin Parsons turbines. The ships carried a complement of 14 officers and 274 men.

The photograph above was taken during one of the summer voyages which the fleet usually made to the Baltic Sea or to Norway. Especially with the establishment of German colonies, ships on foreign service found their duties taking them to all parts of the world. In 1888 landing parties from the *Adler*, *Olga* and *Eber* put down an uprising in Samoa. Between 1888 and 1890 a cruiser squadron with the *Leipzig*, *Carola*, *Sophie*, *Möwe*, *Schwalbe* and *Pfeil* blockaded the German East African coast and, both ashore and at sea, cut off the Arab slave traders in that area. In 1891 the squadron was sent to Chile and in 1893 went for rest and recreation to Cape Town. During the nineties various sorties were made by individual ships protecting German interests in Morocco, Crete, Haiti and Cuba. The occupation of the Bay of Kiaochow Wan and Tsingtao harbour led to the landing of a shore party under Vice-Admiral von Diederichs. A second cruiser division under Prince Heinrich was also sent to East Asia where, in 1900/01, four Brandenburg-Class battleships and four light cruisers were sent to reinforce the international expeditionary force against the Chinese Boxers. In 1902 German cruisers and gun-boats blockaded the Venezuelan coast; in 1904 cruisers were sent with troops to German South-West Africa; in 1905 they were sent to East Africa and in 1911 they were despatched to Ponape in the Caroline Islands in the South Seas.

In 1899 the first ocean-going torpedo-boat was launched at the Schichau yards in Elbing. Unlike the British, Germany's development of the torpedo-boat had long been confined to smaller types, conforming to Tirpitz's tactics of a frontal attack, accompanied by flanking movements to produce a pincer action. The *S90* was the first ship of this new type. This design was heavily influenced by developments in the newer British destroyers, and later ships of this class usually had heavier torpedo strike-power but lighter artillery than their British counterparts.

Starting with the *S90*, these two-funnelled vessels were officially classified as "large torpedo-boats" but, with the later introduction of the 1374-t B-97-Class boats, they were loosely referred to as "destroyers". The *S90* had a displacement of 310 t, was 63 m long and could steam at 27 knots. She was armed with three 5-cm quickfiring cannon and three deck-level torpedo tubes of 45-cm calibre. Subsequently, a total of 48 further ships of this class was launched from the Schichau and Germania yards between 1899 and 1907, gradually increasing in size up to 580 t and 71.5 m in length. They were numbered from 91 to 137 and carried the initial letter of the yards where they were built. They all had identical torpedo strike-power and, at first, the same ordnance. However, from *G132* onwards they carried four 5.2-cm cannon and, from *G135* (commissioned in 1935), an 8.8-cm gun. The *S125* and *G137* were the first to be equipped with turbines; the others were powered by two triple-expansion engines. They had a complement of two officers and 59 men, except for the *G137*, which had 3 officers and 78 men. A number of these ships made names for themselves. The *S90* was beached after sinking a Japanese cruiser off Tsingtao in 1914. The *S97*, painted white instead of the usual black and sailing under the name *Sleipner*, was attached as despatch-boat to the Kaiser's yacht, the *Hohenzollern*. And the *S115*, *S117*, *S118* and *S119*, having lost the *S116* to torpedoes from a British submarine in the North Sea, were engaged by the British cruiser *Undaunted* and four destroyers in a gun battle off the English coast, sinking with a loss of 218 lives.

In 1901, the Navy set up its own torpedo works at Friedrichsort, producing weapons with a maximum range of 3000 m, a speed of 27 knots and a calibre of 45 cm.

Below: One of the first series of Schichau-built ocean-going torpedo-boats, the *S95*.

Right: Battleship *Deutschland*, fleet flagship from 1906 to 1912.

During the years 1903 to 1908 the navy commissioned five Deutschland-Class battleships. They were of 13,191 t displacement, 128 m in length and, with engines identical to those of the Braunschweig Class, could steam at about 19 knots. Their main and secondary armament were also the same, as were the strengths of their crews.

The ship-of-the-line *Deutschland* (Germania yards, 1904) served as flagship for the fleet between 1906 and 1912, took part in the battle of the Jutland in 1916, was used as barracks ship in Wilhelmshaven from 1917 and was broken up in 1922. The *Hannover* (Imperial Shipyard, Wilhelmshaven, 1905) also took part at Jutland. After a rebuild in 1920/21 she served with the fleet until 1935 and was then used as a radio controlled target ship for aircraft. She was finally broken up in Bremerhaven in 1944/46. The *Pommern* (AG. Vulcan, Stettin, 1905) was hit by a torpedo from a British destroyer at Jutland on June 1, 1916, and sank with 839 men. The *Schlesien* (Schichau, Danzig, 1906) also fought at Jutland, became a training ship in 1917, was rebuilt in 1926/27, fought in the Baltic during World War II and, crippled by mines and bombs off Swinemünde in May 1945, was sunk by her crew. The *Schleswig-Holstein* (Germania yards, 1906) also took part at Jutland. In 1917 she was used as barracks ship, became flagship to the fleet during the twenties, took part in the conquest of Poland in 1939 and of Denmark in 1940. In 1944, after serving as a training ship, she was hit by British bombers and sank off Gdynia.

Above: The *Pommern*. Opposite: Ship of the Deutschland Class firing a salute, to starboard.

The Kiel canal, opened in 1895, soon proved almost indispensable to the navy, giving easy access from the main naval base at Kiel into the North Sea. Between 1907 and 1914 the canal was deepened and widened, and the locks enlarged, to permit the

passage of the bigger battleships then being built. Typical of these were the Nassau Class, first launched in 1908.

The top photograph on the opposite page shows the light cruiser *Falke* of the Bussard Class passing under the Levensau Bridge on her return in 1907 from five-and-a-half years of foreign service, including action off Samoa and Venezuela. The middle picture shows the mine-laying cruiser *Nautilus* (AG. Weser, 1907) of 1975 t and 100 m length, and in the bottom picture is the battleship *Kaiser Karl der Grosse*.

Above: The Braunschweig-Class battleship *Hessen* passing under the high-level Grünenthal Bridge.

Right: A view from the *Bellevue* in Kiel of ships of the fleet at anchor in Kiel Harbour in the summer of 1906.

Left: A Deutschland-Class battleship in Kiel Harbour.

Left: The Stettin-Class light cruiser *Stuttgart* (Imperial Shipyard, Danzig, 1906), basically identical to the 1902 Bremen Class but distinguishable by the greater distance between the second and third funnels. The somewhat smaller *Königsberg* (Imperial Shipyard, Kiel, 1905), after service with the fleet, took part in the blockade of the Rufiji delta in East Africa and, heavily damaged by British warships, was scuttled by her crew in July 1915. The *Nürnberg* (Imperial Shipyard, Kiel, 1906), pictured bottom left, also belonged to the Stettin Class. She was with von Spee's cruiser squadron in the battle of the Falkland Islands when, in December 1914, she was sunk with 327 men. Yet another Stettin-Class ship was the

Stettin herself, handed over to Great Britain in 1920, after service with the fleet, and there broken up for scrap. She was launched from the Vulcan yards in Stettin in 1907.

The next series of light cruisers were the two Dresden-Class ships pictured below. They were the *Dresden* (centre) and the *Emden* (right). They had a displacement of 3664 t and were 118 m long. The *Dresden*, powered by twin Parsons turbines, ran at 25 knots. She carried the standard armament of a Stettin-Class vessel and had a complement of 18 officers and 343 men.

The *Dresden* (Blohm & Voss, 1907) fought at the Battle of Coronel in 1914 and also at the Falkland Islands, from which she was the only German survivor. However, in March of the following year she was crippled by gunfire from British ships in a bay of the Chilean island of Mas a Tierra and was scuttled by her crew. The *Emden* (Imperial Shipyard, Danzig, 1908) fared somewhat better. Released from von Spee's cruiser squadron in East Asia in 1914, she became the terror of the Allied trade routes in the Indian Ocean until, in November of that year, after a battle with the British light cruiser *Sydney*, she was beached in the Cocos Islands and lay there until 1950, when she was finally broken up.

At the beginning of the nineties even the heaviest warships held fire with their forward guns until they had closed to a range of 3000 m. Their main firepower still lay in a concentrated "broadside" of medium artillery at a range of 500 to 1000 m. The first real change came with the Brandenburg Class, their 28-cm turret-mounted forward and rear guns giving a range of up to 15 km. At this time, too, Admiral Thomsen was appointed Inspector of Gunnery, and he began a systematic research programme which resulted in major improvements in naval weaponry, especially heavy artillery, and also had considerable effect on the design of ships then being built. The destruction of the Russian fleet during the Battle of Tsushima in 1905, by Japanese naval gunners using German artillery tactics, provided an object lesson for the British, who in 1906 launched the first of their battleships with all big guns—the *Dreadnought*.

In 1908 the first German Dreadnought was launched from the Imperial Shipyard at Wilhelmshaven. She was the *Nassau*, the first dreadnought-battleship of the German Navy. She had a displacement of 18,873 t and was 146 m long. Like ships of the Deutschland Class, with their turrets fore and aft, the *Nassau* had such twin turrets with 28-cm guns. She also carried two twin gun turrets on either side, all with 28-cm rapid-loading cannon. This gave her a total of twelve guns of heavier calibre than ever before and she carried, in addition, twelve 15-cm and sixteen 8.8-cm cannon and six torpedo tubes. Her three triple-expansion engines and three screws gave her a speed of 20 knots. She had a complement of 40 officers and 968 men. The four ships of the Nassau Class formed the Navy's first battleship division in 1910. They all took part in the Battle of Jutland.

Right: Cruising in line astern (left to right), the *Nassau*, *Westfalen*, *Rheinland*, *Posen* and two battleships of the Deutschland Class.

Right: The *Nassau* at high speed in the Baltic. She was handed over to Japan in 1920 and broken up in Holland.

Rigth: The *Westfalen* (AG. Weser, 1908). She was handed over to Great Britain in 1920 and broken up.

Below: The *Nassau* and the *Westfalen* follow six ships from the Second Battle-Squadron out of Kiel harbour.

Above: The *Rheinland* (foreground) and a sister ship of the Nassau Class during manoeuvres in a heavy sea. The *Rheinland* (AG. Vulcan, Stettin, 1908) ran aground on the Aland Islands during a fog in April 1918, but was refloated; later she surrendered to the Allies, and was broken up in 1921 in Holland. Left: The *Posen* (Germania, 1908) was handed over at the same time and broken up in Dordrecht.

Left: The large cruiser *Hertha* of the Viktoria-Luise Class, built 1897, after her rebuild in 1906/08 with her original three funnels reduced to two.

Right: Mine-layer *Albatross*, sister ship of the *Nautilus*, launched from the AG. Weser yards in Bremen in 1907.

Left: The light cruiser *Kolberg* (Schichau, Danzig, 1908). She was surrendered to France in 1920 and served with the French Navy under the name *Colmar* until 1927.

Right: The armoured cruiser *Blücher*, launched from the Imperial Shipyard in Kiel in 1908.

The armoured cruisers (which differed from previous cruisers in being heavily armoured) were also steadily increasing in size and armament. The two sister ships launched in 1906, the *Scharnhorst* (Blohm & Voss) and the *Gneisenau* (AG. Weser), already had displacements of 11,616 t, lengths of 144.6 m and speeds of 23.5 knots. They carried eight 21-cm, six 15-cm and eighteen 8.8-cm quickfiring cannon as well as four torpedo tubes. Both belonged to Vice-Admiral Graf von Spee's cruiser squadron, and both were lost off the Falkland Islands in December 1914 with 1,458 men. Next in this series was the *Blücher* (Imperial Shipyard, Kiel, 1908) with a displacement of 15,842 t, a length of 161.8 m and a speed of just under 26 knots. Her twelve 21-cm guns were mounted in pairs, in a similar disposition to those of the Nassau-Class vessels, in heavily armoured gun turrets. This arrangement foreshadowed the development, a year later, of a series of even bigger armoured cruisers, starting with the *Von der Tann,* which were then named "battle cruisers".

The *Blücher,* with 792 men, was lost in January 1915 in an engagement with British battle-cruisers in the North Sea.

During 1907/09 two cruisers were built especially equipped as mine-layers. They were the *Nautilus,* of 1974 t, and the 2208 t *Albatross,* both with a length of 100 m. They carried 200 mines and were armed with eight 8.8-cm guns. The *Nautilus* ended her days as a prison ship and was eventually scrapped. The *Albatross,* heavily damaged by Russian cruisers, was beached in Gottland in 1915, salvaged and interned in Sweden and finally broken up in Hamburg in 1921. Amongst other mine-layers were the sister ships *Brummer* and *Bremse* (AG. Vulcan, 1915/16) of 4385 t and carrying 400 mines each. They were interned at Scapa Flow in 1918.

Although still practically unarmoured, the light cruisers too were getting steadily bigger. Compared with the 4362-t, 118-m *Kolberg* (1908), the last of this series, the Cöln-Class light cruisers launched at the Imperial Shipyards in 1918, were 155 m long and had a displacement of 5620 t. This series consisted of the Kolberg-Class ships launched between 1908 and 1909: the *Kolberg, Mainz, Cöln* and *Augsburg;* the 1911 class of *Magdeburg, Breslau, Strassburg* and *Stralsund* (see page 141); the 1912-class *Karlsruhe* and *Rostock* (page 141); the sister ships *Graudenz* (1913) and *Regensburg* (1914); the sister ships *Wiesbaden* and *Frankfurt* (1915); the 1915/16 class *Königsberg, Karlsruhe, Emden* and *Nürnberg* and the *Cöln* (see page 156) and the *Dresden* (1916 and 1917 respectively). The latter two were each in a class of their own, bringing the total number of classes in the series up to ten.

Below: Battleships of the Helgoland Class in line ahead. From left to right: *Oldenburg, Ostfriesland, Helgoland* and *Thüringen.*

Overleaf: Battleship *Deutschland* (right) and the light cruiser *Hela* during a summer visit to Balholm in Norway's Esefjord in 1910.

Of the light cruisers launched from 1909 onwards, the *Mainz* and the first *Cöln* were lost in battle in the North Sea in 1914 and went down with 596 men. The *Magdeburg* was sunk in the Baltic in the same year with a loss of 15 lives. The *Breslau*, sailing as the Turkish *Midilli*, went down with 330 men in the Aegean in January 1918; the *Wiesbaden*, with 588 men aboard, including the poet and writer Gorch Fock, was sunk at Jutland. After the Armistice the remaining light cruisers were either handed over to the Allies or, as in most cases, interned at Scapa Flow.

The battleships of the Helgoland Class built between 1908 and 1912, with their 22,808-t displacement, 167-m length and twelve 30.5-cm guns mounted in pairs in turrets, had already essentially overtaken the Nassau-Class dreadnoughts. The first three were launched in 1909: the *Helgoland* from the Howaldts yards in Kiel; the *Ostfriesland* (see page 153) from the Imperial Shipyard in Wilhelmshaven, and the *Thüringen* from AG. Weser in Bremen. In 1910 the *Oldenburg* was launched at Schichau in Danzig. They all took part in the Battle of Jutland. After World War I the *Helgoland* was handed over to Great Britain, the *Ostfriesland* to the USA, the *Thüringen* to France and the *Oldenburg* to Japan. They were broken up between 1921 and 1924.

Left: Ocean-going torpedo-boats execute a textbook breakthrough manoeuvre during naval exercises.

New series of larger torpedo-boats were launched between 1906 and 1911 from Schichau in Elbing, Vulcan in Stettin and the Germania yards in Kiel. They were numbered from 138 to 197, prefixed by the initial letter of the yard where they were built. Like the *S90* series built from 1899 onwards, they had two funnels. From the *V161* (1908) onwards, they were all turbine-powered. The earlier boats had a displacement of 533 t and a length of 71 m; this was later increased to 660 t and 74 m. They were capable of speeds between 30 and 34 knots. They mounted originally one, later two 8.8-cm quickfiring cannon and were later re-armed with either one or two 10.5-cm quickfiring cannon as well as smaller machine-guns. They carried three deck-level 45-cm calibre torpedo tubes, later increased, from the *G174* onwards, to four of the new 50-cm calibre.

With the launching in 1911, from the Vulcan yards in Stettin, of the 569-t *v1*, a new numbering system was introduced. The yard initials of the earlier boats were replaced with the series number "T", although only the last two digits appeared on their bows. The *T183* (ex-*V183*) thus carried only the number "83". After the 1911 V1 Class, the next series of heavy torpedo-boats were the V25 Class (1914) of 812 to 916 t; the B97 Class (1914) which, with three funnels and a 1843-t displacement, were the first officially-named "destroyers"; the G96 (1916) Class of 890 to 924 t; and the *S113* and the *V116* (1918), which were the only two vessels of the S113 Class to be completed. These last two had a displacement of 2060 t, a length of 106 m, made 36 knots and were armed with four 15-cm guns. In World War I they were the largest destroyers of any of the seapowers.

As well as the ocean-going torpedo-boats and destroyers a number of smaller torpedo-boats of the "A" series were built during World War I, originally intended as support craft for action off the coast of Flanders. They had displacements of 109 t (*A1* to *A25*, 1915 onwards), 227 t (*A26* to *A55*, 1916) and 330 t (*A56* to *A113*, 1917/1918) and had only a single funnel (see page 160).

During World War I the ocean-going boats took part in almost every naval action in the North Sea and the Baltic, especially in the Baltic provinces. They served as coastguards and convoy escorts; relatively few were lost. After the war they were mostly broken up for scrap, although the newer ones were surrendered to the Allies. A few of the older boats were taken over by the New Navy. During the Battle of Jutland *V4*, *V27*, *V29*, *S35* and *V48* were sunk.

Below: large torpedo-boats (with *V183* in the foreground) break through a line of Nassau-Class battleships during manoeuvres.

Right: The torpedo-boat *S144* at high speed.

In 1909 the large armoured cruiser *Von der Tann* was launched at Blohm & Voss in Hamburg. She had a displacement of 19,370 t, was 171 m long, and her twin Parsons turbines drove her at 27.4 knots. She was armed with eight 28-cm guns mounted in pairs in four turrets, ten 15-cm and sixteen 8.8-cm guns, and four torpedo tubes. She was the first German battle-cruiser and the first turbine-powered heavy German fighting-ship. She took part at Jutland and was interned in 1918 at Scapa Flow. Blohm & Voss also built her sister ships, the *Moltke* (1910) and the *Goeben* (1911), both somewhat larger at 22,979 t (see page 142) and, in 1912, the even larger *Seydlitz* of 24,988 t displacement and 200 m length. The *Moltke* fought at Dogger Bank and Jutland and was interned at Scapa Flow in 1918. The *Goeben* was taken over by the Turkish Navy in August 1914 and, under the name *Jawuz Sultan Selim*, served long after the end of the Second World War. The *Seydlitz* served as flagship to the Fleet Scouting Forces. Heavily damaged at Jutland, she managed to return to Wilhelmshaven.

Above: Ocean-going torpedo-boats *V162*, *V164*, *S139*, *G132* and *V163* in harbour.
Left: The battle-cruiser *Von der Tann*.
Right: The two after turrets of the battle-cruiser *Goeben*.
Overleaf: The fleet during a summer visit to Heligoland in 1913. The *Ostfriesland* (left), the fleet flagship *Friedrich der Grosse* (centre) and, to the right of her, four ships of the Deutschland and Braunschweig Class.

Left: The battleship *Kaiser* (Imperial Shipyard, Kiel, 1911), the first of the new Kaiser Class (see page 143), to which the other ships shown below, and the *Prinzregent Luitpold,* also belonged.

Left: The battleship *Friedrich der Grosse* (Vulcan, Hamburg, 1911), from 1912 to 1916 flagship to the fleet.

Left: The battleship *Kaiserin* (Howaldts yards, Kiel, 1911).

Left: The battleship *König Albert* (Schichau, Danzig, 1912).

Right: The light cruiser *Strassburg* (Imperial Shipyard, Wilhelmshaven, 1910/12) of the Magdeburg Class. She was handed over to Italy in 1920 and, under the name *Taranto*, sunk by Allied bombers during World War II.

Right: The light cruiser *Stralsund* (Imperial Shipyard, Wilhelmshaven, 1910/12), also of the Magdeburg Class. She was surrendered to France in 1920 and, under the name *Mulhouse*, served with the French Navy until 1935.

Right: The light cruiser *Karlsruhe* (Germania yards, Kiel, 1911/14), after harrying the trade routes of the Mid-Atlantic, went down with 263 men in November 1914 after an explosion, east of Trinidad.

Right: The light cruiser *Rostock* (Howaldts yard, Kiel, 1911/14) was sunk at Jutland with a loss of 14 men.

Right: Battle-cruiser *Moltke* under full steam in the North Sea.

Left: Battle-cruiser *Seydlitz* heads out of Kiel Harbour.

Right: König-Class battleship, the *König,* launched 1913 at the Imperial Shipyard, Wilhelmshaven.

Left: Derfflinger-Class battle-cruiser, the *Hindenburg* (Imperial Shipyard, Wilhelmshaven, 1913).
Right: Battle-cruiser *Derfflinger* (Blohm & Voss, Hamburg, 1913).

The Kaiser-Class ships which followed the Helgoland Class were even bigger. They displaced 24,724 t, were 172 m long, had triple screws and were the first turbine-driven battleships with oil-fired boilers. The third ship in this class, the *Prinzregent Luitpold*, became the first to be fitted out with the new marine diesel engines. Their armament was similar to that of the Helgoland Class but they had only ten 30.5-cm guns. For the first time the rear gun turrets were arranged in two tiers, one above and slightly forward of the other. They had a complement of 41 officers and 1043 men. All five ships of this class were launched during 1912/13. Except for the *König Albert* they all fought at Jutland, with the *Friedrich der Grosse* serving as Commander-in-Chief Vice-Admiral Scheer's flagship. In 1918 all were interned in Scapa Flow.

The next series of König-Class ships were the *König* (Imperial Shipyard, Wilhelmshaven, 1913); the *Grosser Kurfürst* (AG. Vulcan, Hamburg, 1913); the *Markgraf* (AG. Weser, Bremen, 1913) and the *Kronprinz*, later renamed the *Kronprinz Wilhelm* in January 1918 (Germania yards, Kiel, 1914). They displaced 25,796 t, were 175 m long, made 21 knots and were armed similarly to the ships of the Kaiser-Class but, for the first time, had gun turrets mounted amidships. They carried 41 officers and 1095 men. All these ships, in 1918, were interned at Scapa Flow.

The last ships in this series to join the Kaiser's navy were two of the originally planned four Bayern-Class battleships. They were both completed during the war, the *Bayern* at Howaldts yards, Kiel, and the *Baden* at Schichau in Danzig (see page 157). They were of 28,600 t and were 180 m long. Their three sets of turbines gave them a speed of 22 knots. They mounted two-tiered twin gun turrets fore and aft, with eight 38-cm guns, and also had sixteen 15-cm guns, two 8.8-cm anti-aircraft guns and five of the new 60-cm calibre torpedo tubes. From October 1916 onwards the *Baden* became the last of the Kaiser's fleet flagships; the *Bayern* took part in the invasion of the Baltic Islands. Both were interned at Scapa Flow in 1918.

Also completed during the war were the last of the Kaiser's battle-cruisers: The *Derfflinger* (Blohm & Voss, 1913); *Lützow* (Schichau, Danzig, 1913) and the *Hindenburg* (Imperial Shipyard, Wilhelmshaven, 1915). They had a displacement of just under 27,000 t and were from 210 to 212 m long. They were capable of speeds up to 27 knots, and their heavy armament consisted of eight 30.5-cm guns. The *Lützow* went down at Jutland; her two sister ships were interned at Scapa Flow. Other battle-cruisers were projected but never built. These would have been the Mackensen and the Yorck Classes, the design of the latter having influence on the battleships *Scharnhorst* and *Gneisenau* built during the thirties.

The first German submarine was designed and built at the Germania yards in Kiel. She was launched in 1906 and, in September of that year, entered service as the *U1*. She displaced 238 t on the surface, 283 t submerged, and was 42 m long. Her gasoline engines gave her a surface speed of 11 knots; under water, on her batteries, she could make 8.7 knots. She was used mainly as a research and training vessel, was retired in 1919 and today stands on display at the Deutsches Museum in Munich. After her, in 1909, came the *U3* and *U4* of 421 t, both from the Imperial Shipyard at Danzig, and, until the outbreak of the war, the two yards produced between them *U8* to *U35*. From the *U19* onwards they were diesel-powered, with displacements on the surface of between 650 and 680 t. They were usually equipped with four torpedo tubes. Guns, usually a single 8.8-cm cannon, were only installed after the beginning of the war.

The four original submarines were formed in 1910 into the First U-Boat Flotilla; at the same time a U-boat training centre was established at Kiel, together with the formation of a submariners' company. It was not until well after the start of World War I that the submarine was to become the main strike weapon of the navy, due mainly to the steady development of the "medium U-boat" of approximately 750 to 800 t and 65 m length. The war years also saw the construction of small *UB*-Type coastal U-boats of around 300 to 500 t displacement and lengths between 35 and 55 m, mine-laying submarines, and one or two larger cruiser submarines of 2000 t displacement which were barely launched before the war ended. A total of 343 U-boats was put into service during World War I. Of these, 178 were lost in action, seven were interned in neutral harbours and 14 were blown up at the end of the war. Of their crews, 5132 lost their lives—more than half of their total manpower. German U-boats sank 5861 ships during the war, along with an unknown number of seamen.

Below: The first German U-boats during an Imperial Review off Danzig in 1910: the *U1* to *U6*, *U9* and *U10*.

The above painting by Willy Stöwer shows
the fleet Review before the Kaiser in 1912.
In the centre, the Royal Yacht *Hohenzollern* from whose signal bridge Kaiser Wilhelm II takes the salute. In the foreground,
the *U1*. The crews of the ships at anchor
stand at "eyes front".

Above: A U-boat flotilla. In the foreground the *U15* (Imperial Shipyard, Danzig, 1911) of 516 t surface displacement and 58 m length. She was rammed by the British cruiser *Birmingham* in the North Sea in August 1914 and sank with her entire crew.

Opposite: A photograph taken during a Mediterranean sortie in World War I on the *U35*. On the left, her commander, Lieutenant de la Perrière. The *U35* was launched at the Germania yards in Kiel in 1914. She displaced 685 t and was 65 m long. For a time she served with the Austrian Navy and was handed over to Great Britain in 1918.

Overleaf: The Battle of Jutland, from a painting by Claus Bergen which now hangs at the Naval College, Mürwik. The line of battleships under Vice-Admiral Scheer, led by four König-Class battleships, exchanges fire with Admiral Jellicoe's British ships.

Following: The heavy torpedo-boat *S18* (Imperial Shipyard, Wilhelmshaven, 1912). She served off the coast of Flanders and elsewhere during the war and later with the Reich Navy until 1931.

CLAUS BERGE
MÜNCHEN

Above: The battleship *Friedrich der Grosse,* from a painting by Alex Kircher. In the foreground, an ocean-going torpedo-boat; in the background, a light cruiser.

The assassination in Sarajevo, with its immediate threat of war, took place on June 28 1914. It coincided with the annual Kiel week, which was attended, as usual, by the Kaiser. The visiting British warships, like their German counterparts, lowered their flags to half-mast as a mark of sorrow and respect for the murdered heir to the German throne. They departed, two days later, with the signal: "Friends today, friends in the future, friends forever". Within a month, the friendship was laid aside. War had been declared.

At the time, the German fleet consisted of 14 of the most modern battleships, 16 older battleships, four battle-cruisers, 9 armourd, 6 large and 34 light cruisers, 90 torpedo boats and 21 U-boats. Except for the *Goeben,* all the modern heavy ships were in German waters. The war at sea with Great Britain started at the end of August with a battle off Helgoland; in January 1915, with most of the German Navy engaged in Baltic operations,

German and British ships met at Dogger Bank.

In February of 1917 German U-boats were ordered into unlimited war against Allied shipping. The Navy was in action on all fronts, striking deep into enemy waters, on coastal patrols and mine-laying missions. But the battle for which they had waited—for which preparations and training had long been in hand—did not come until the end of May 1916. This was the Battle of Jutland, in which almost all the heavy ships of the Navy took part. On May 31 and June 1, more than a hundred thousand men on 247 ships stood facing each other. From this battle, 14 English ships—a total of 115,025 t—and 6094 men never returned. German losses were 11 ships (61,180 t total) and 2551 men. The German Navy fought brilliantly but—as things turned out—to no avail.

Below: A view across the decks of the *Ostfriesland* as the Third Squadron pushes into the North Sea.

The East Asian Cruiser Squadron under Graf Spee, with the *Scharnhorst, Gneisenau, Nürnberg* and *Emden*, which were later released on lone service missions, sailed to South America after the outbreak of war where they joined up with the *Dresden* and the *Leipzig* at Easter Island. On November 1, off Coronel, they met and sank two British armoured cruisers; then, rounding the Horn, they set course for home. Off the Falkland Islands, on December 8 1914, they encountered a superior force of English warships. From the battle that followed, only the *Dresden* escaped. However, in March 1915, she was caught by British cruisers in Cumberland Bay in the neutral island of Mas a Tierra and, badly damaged by gunfire, was scuttled by her crew.

Right: The cruiser squadron under Vice-Admiral Graf Spee; a photograph taken on December 2 as the ships round the Horn in heavy seas.

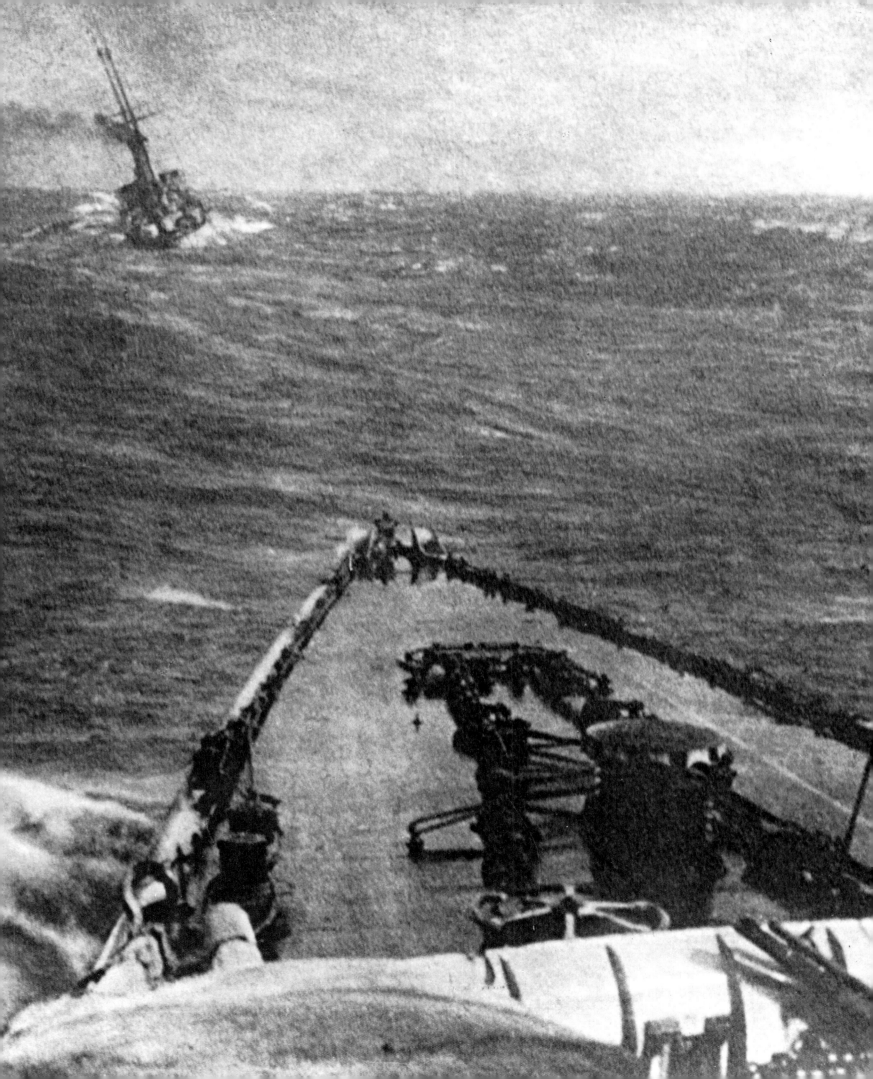

In February 1915 Admiral von Pohl, until then chief of the Admiralty Staff, relieved Admiral von Ingenohl as Commander of the Fleet, his own position being taken over by Admiral Bachmann. Pohl retired due to ill-health in January of the following year and, a month later, died. He was succeeded by Vice-Admiral Scheer. Admiral of the Fleet von Tirpitz (who had been titled by the Kaiser in 1900), in protest against what to him seemed an over-cautious use of the U-boat as a strike weapon, resigned his command in March 1916.

Apart from a few ships engaged in the North Sea and the Baltic, the main strength of the German Navy spent the months following the Battle of Jutland lying at anchor in Wilhelmshaven and Kiel. With the war practically lost, sailors in the main fleet mutinied. It was their rising in Kiel which led to the November Revolution of 1918, and the end of the Kaiser's Empire.

Left: The light cruiser *Cöln*, built during 1915/18 at Blohm & Voss in Hamburg.

Right: The battleship *Baden,* flying the admiral's flag, at full speed. Built at Schichau in Danzig during 1913/16, she was the last fleet flagship of the Kaiser's navy.

Left: An aerial photograph of part of the fleet at anchor in Kiel Harbour during the First World War. From front to rear, a battleship of the Ostfriesland Class, a ship of the Nassau Class, another Ostfriesland-Class ship, and three light cruisers.

Below: An aerial photograph taken at about the same time, also in Kiel. In the front row, right to left: the light cruiser *Strassburg;* the battleships *König, Kronprinz* and *Bayern,* and two other battleships of the König-Class.

Overleaf: Part of the fleet at anchor in Wilhelmshaven in 1918: to the left, a battleship of the Kaiser-Class; in the background, cruisers and battleships; to the right, torpedo-boats.

Left: The *M81* (Seebeck yards, Geeste-münde, 1919). She served during World War II as the *M581* and, after the capitulation in 1945, under the British-controlled German Minesweeping Administration.
Below: One of the torpedo-boats of the *A68—A79* series, primarily engaged on the Flanders coast.
Right: Two of the vessels left to the reconstituted German Navy in 1922 after the Treaty of Versailles: a light cruiser (left) and an ocean-going torpedo-boat.

During the war the Navy requisitioned a great many vessels of all kinds for service as auxiliary craft. The most important of these was a series of freighters and passenger ships which were converted into auxiliary cruisers. Trawlers were also requisitioned and usually served as patrol ships for picket work. From 1915 onwards, the smaller German shipbuilding yards set to work producing minesweepers, of an average 500-t displacement, 60-m length and capable of speeds of around 16 knots. The immediate postwar years found these craft busily employed in the thickly strewn minefields. They carried series numbers from *M1* to *M176* although a few of them (from *M139* onwards) were never completed. Twenty-nine of these vessels were lost during the war, some were sold for scrap in 1920 and the rest were taken over by the Reichsmarine.

The Reichsmarine 1919–1935

The revolution broke out in Berlin on the 9th of November; the Kaiser abdicated and, on the following day, fled to Holland. The First World War ended with the Armistice on November 11. The German Navy totalled its losses; one old battleship (the *Pommern*); one battle-cruiser (the *Lützow*); 6 armoured and 18 light cruisers; 10 gunboats; 107 torpedo-boats and destroyers; 198 U-boats; 29 minesweepers; 5 unclassified ships; 17 auxiliary cruisers; 170 auxiliary craft; 30 airships and 170 aircraft. Under the terms of the Armistice, Germany gave up her entire U-boat fleet, disarmed her main fleet and handed over its

control. Nearly 150 of the newer ships were interned in Scapa Flow in the Orkney Islands. On June 21, 1919, at the end of the Armistice and a week before the peace treaty was signed, the commanding officer, Rear-Admiral Reuter, ordered all ships at Scapa Flow to be sunk. The Versailles Treaty left the German Reich with six old battleships, six cruisers, 24 torpedo-boats and a number of lighter craft.

At the beginning of 1919 most of the men still under orders to the navy were demobilised. On the 26th of March, Scheer's former chief of staff, Rear-Admiral von Trotha, was appointed head of the newly formed

Admiralty, now in supreme command of the Navy. In April, the National Assembly at Weimar set the seal on plans for the future development of the German Navy with its assent to proposals for the construction of new naval bases at Wilhelmshaven on the North Sea and Kiel in the Baltic. After a year, Trotha was replaced by Vice-Admiral Michaelis who soon was followed in turn by Admiral Behncke. Admirals Zenker and Raeder followed as chiefs of the Admiralty in 1924 and 1928, respectively. In March 1921 the Reichstag passed the service regulations which established the Reich Navy.

On January 1 1922 the old battle-flag of the Reich was replaced with a new one. Instead of the black, red and gold, the new flag was black, white and red, in horizontal stripes of equal width. The inset of the Kaiser's Navy was replaced by an Iron Cross with an edging of black, red and gold. The use of this flag was discontinued by order of the President of the Reich, von Hindenburg, on March 14 1933, after the National Socialist party seized power.

The first major task facing the Reich's navy was the clearing of the mines left over from the war. More than 300 minesweepers were detailed to this operation, which was only completed in October of 1922.

In 1924, the cruiser *Berlin*, originally built in 1915 as a gunboat but later converted to the survey ship *Meteor*, and three of the remaining old battleships, went on the first overseas missions since the war. These voyages served primarily as training missions, giving their crews practical experience and helping to put the Navy once more on a war footing.

In 1925, at what had once been the Imperial Shipyard in Wilhelmshaven but had since been renamed the Reich Naval Yards, the first of the Navy's new ships ran down the slipway. She was the light cruiser *Emden*, of 6056 t displacement and 155 m length (see page 164). She was powered by two sets of oil-fired turbines and ran at 29.4 knots. She was armed with eight 15-cm guns and four torpedo tubes, and carried a complement of 19 officers and 464 men. Rebuilt during the thirties, the *Emden* took part in the invasion of Norway and, in 1945, transported refugees from Pillau near Kaliningrad to Kiel. There, badly damaged by bombs on May 3, she was beached and blown up by her crew.

Left: Originally a Danish freighter, the *Niobe* was rebuilt in 1913 and, in 1923, was taken over as a training ship. She went down in a storm in July of that year and was lost with 69 men.

Right: Ship-of-the-line *Schlesien* after her rebuild in 1927.

The next light cruisers to be built were those of the Königsberg Class: the *Königsberg* (see page 169), *Karlsruhe* and *Köln* (see page 165). These were launched during 1927/28. They had a displacement of 7210 t, a length of 174 m and were driven by two oil-fired turbines, with two auxiliary diesel engines, which gave them speeds of around 32 knots. The *Karlsruhe* was built at the Deutsche Werke in Kiel.

Until 1935 she served as a training ship, then with the fleet. During the Norwegian campaign in April 1940 she was hit by three British torpedoes off Kristiansand and was sunk by her crew. The last series of German light cruisers, the sister ships *Leipzig* (see page 164) and *Nürnberg* (see page 172), were of the same size as the Königsberg-Class ships, and made roughly the same speeds. Their armament was also similar:

two triple turrets aft and one forward, each mounting three 15-cm guns. Unlike the earlier vessels with their two funnels, the latter two had only one.

Below: The torpedo-boats *Albatros* and *Kondor*, built 1925/28, break through the line during naval manoeuvres. The photograph was taken from the old battleship *Schleswig-Holstein*.

Left: The light cruiser *Emden* after her modernization in 1938.

Left: The light cruiser *Königsberg* (Naval Yards, Wilhelmshaven, 1925/26). She served with the fleet after 1936, as gunnery training ship. She was bombed during the Norwegian invasion in 1940 and sank off Bergen.

Left: The light cruiser *Leipzig* (Naval Yards, Wilhelmshaven, 1929). She served off Spain in 1936/38, took part in the Baltic Islands campaign in 1941 and off Danzig in 1945. In 1946 she was loaded with ex-World War II poison-gas canisters and sunk in the North Sea.

Right: The light cruiser *Köln* (Naval Yards, Wilhelmshaven, 1928). She served with the fleet until 1939, took part in the Norwegian invasion and was sunk by Allied bombers in Wilhelmshaven in 1945.

The photograph on the left shows the launching of the *Deutschland* at Deutsche Werke, Kiel in May 1931. Due to the restrictions imposed on Germany by the peace treaty, development work was concentrated on ships of this type. The *Deutschland* represented a cruiser, more heavily armed than her counterparts of similar size, yet capable of speeds greater than those of the larger and more heavily armed warships of other powers. This, the first of the "pocket battleships", was followed by two of the same type: the *Admiral Graf Spee* and the *Admiral Scheer*, launched during 1933/34 at the Reich Naval Yards in Wilhelmshaven. These ships displaced around 12,000 t, were from 186 to 188 m long and, with marine diesels, made a little over 28 knots. They had a triple gun turret fore and aft, mounting a total of six 28-cm guns. In addition, they carried eight 15-cm and three 8.8-cm anti-aircraft guns and eight torpedo tubes mounted in sets of four. The *Deutschland* was mainly on foreign service until 1939, was damaged by a bomb off Ibiza during the Spanish Civil War in 1937, attacked Allied merchant shipping in the Atlantic in 1939, was renamed the Heavy Cruiser *Lützow* in 1940, took part in the invasion of Norway and, hit by bombs in April 1945, sank off Swinemünde.

Centre left: The forward 28-cm triple gun turret of the *Deutschland*.

Bottom left: The pocket battleship *Admiral Graf Spee* carried out several successful overseas missions and, after suffering shell hits from British cruisers, was scuttled by her crew in the River Plate estuary.

Right: The pocket battleship *Admiral Scheer* took part, with her sister ships, in the Spanish Civil War. In 1940, classified as a heavy cruiser, she harried Allied shipping in the Atlantic and Indian Oceans. In 1942 she was stationed in Norway and, in March 1945, transported refugees from East Prussia to Kiel. In April, heavily damaged by bombs in Kiel Harbour, she capsized.

Overleaf: From left to right, the *Admiral Scheer, Admiral Graf Spee, Deutschland, Köln, Königsberg* and *Karlsruhe* fire a salute in Kiel Harbour on the twentieth anniversary of the Battle of Jutland, in May 31 1936.

The Kriegsmarine 1935–1945

In 1933 the National Socialists took over the government of Germany. In their general rearmament programme were plans for a considerably strengthened navy—plans which were already being put into effect, in defiance of the articles of the Versailles Treaty, at the time of the Anglo-German naval agreement in 1935. The Reich Navy—the "Reichsmarine"—was renamed, in May 1935, the "Kriegsmarine" (literally, the "War Navy"). In 1936 the command of the navy was placed in the hands of the newly constituted High Command of the Kriegsmarine under Admiral Raeder, whose service rank was the equivalent of an admiral of the fleet. In the same year a new battle-flag was introduced. It showed a white disc charged with a black swastika on a field of red quartered by a black Balkan Cross, with a small Iron Cross in the upper hoist canton.

The *Bremse*, of 1435 t and 104 m length, and the *Brummer* (see page 172) of 2410 t and 113 m length, were two gunnery training ships and mine-layers which were launched from the Naval Yards, Wilhelmshaven in 1931, and at Deschimag in Bremen in 1935 respectively. They both took part in the invasion of Norway where, on April 14 1940, the *Brummer* was sunk in the Kattegat Strait. In September 1941, the *Bremse* was sunk in a battle with British cruisers off the Norwegian coast.

In 1933, as a replacement for the sunken *Niobe*, the fully-rigged barque *Gorch Fock* ran down the slips at the Blohm & Voss yards in Hamburg. Designed as a training ship, she had a displacement of 1354 t and was 74 m long at the waterline. She carried 1800 square metres of sail, with an auxiliary diesel engine. The *Gorch Fock* set the pattern for two slightly larger vessels, the 1634-t, 89-m barques *Horst Wessel* and *Albert Leo Schlageter,* also built by Blohm & Voss during the years 1936/37. They were used as training ships until the end of the war and still exist today: the *Gorch Fock* as the USSR training ship the *Towarischtsch;* the *Horst Wessel* as the American Coast Guard training ship the *Eagle,* and the *Albert Leo Schlageter* as the Portuguese training ship *Sagres.*

Below: The *Gorch Fock* (left) and the *Horst Wessel.*

Right: Outward bound, the crew of the *Gorch Fock* parade in the shrouds.

Left: The light cruiser *Nürnberg* (Deutsche Werke, Kiel, 1934). She served in the Spanish Civil War in 1936/37 and, in March 1939, in the occupation of Memel. She was handed over to Russia after the war and served as the training ship *Admiral Makarow*.

Left: The artillery training ship and minelayer *Brummer*.

Left: The heavy cruiser *Blücher* (Deutsche Werke, Kiel, 1937). On April 9, 1940, after severe damage by Norwegian coastal batteries, she sank in the Dröbak Narrows in the Oslofjord.

Right: One of the Type-IX U-boats built at the Deschimag yards in Bremen between 1936/40. She had a surface displacement of about 1000 t.

In June 1935 the first of the Kriegsmarine's U-boats, the *U1*, was launched at Deutsche Werke, Kiel. She belonged to the type II A and had a surface displacement of 254 t and a length of 41 m. Over forty boats of the similar types II A, II B, II C, and II D followed up to the year 1940, their designs still based largely on those of the UB II- and UF-Type vessels of World War I. By the end of 1935, 14 of these "small" submarines had been taken into service, the first six as training vessels. These and a further eight boats constituted the Weddigen U-boat Flotilla, whose commander (later chief of the submarine arm) was Captain Dönitz. Before the outbreak of war, a few further boats of 626 t surface displacement (275 t submerged) were built. These were the Type-VII U-boats which, later improved as the Types VII B and VII C, were to be built in large numbers for the Atlantic campaign. The Type VII C had five torpedo tubes and 8.8-cm and 2-cm anti-aircraft guns. For long distance missions, the Type IX, with a displacement of about 1000 t, was built. Of these, the *U37* to *U44* were completed by the start of the war. The most effective new types built during the war were the Type XXI of 1623 t and the Type XXIII of 232 t surface displacement. Out of a total of 1170 U-boats, 684 were lost by enemy action during the war, 215 were blown up by their crews when the war ended, and 153 were surrendered afterwards.

Right: Submarines *U7* to *U11* of the Weddigen U-boat Flotilla in harbour.

Below: Type II B U-boats during diving exercises in 1936.
Right: A detail from a painting by Claus Bergen at Mürwik Naval College showing a Type IX B U-boat.

Right: Bow view of the battleship *Scharnhorst*. During early 1941 she attacked merchant shipping in the North Atlantic; in February 1943, took part in the breakthrough in the English Channel and, in December of the same year, in a battle with British warships, sank off the North Cape with 1803 men.

Left: The battleship *Gneisenau,* her rear triple gun turret swung to starboard and clearly visible.

The first heavy cruisers of the Kriegsmarine were the sister ships *Admiral Hipper* (Blohm & Voss, Hamburg, 1937) and *Blücher* (Deutsche Werke, Kiel, 1937). They displaced over 14,000 t (although the officially-declared figure was only 10,000), were 203 m long and, with three sets of turbines, sailed at 32.5 knots. Armament consisted of eight 20.3-cm and twelve 10.5-cm guns, and twelve 3.7-cm anti-aircraft guns (the *Admiral Hipper* was later fitted with twenty-eight 2-cm AA guns in addition) and twelve torpedo tubes. They could also carry three aircraft. They had a complement of 51 officers and, including anti-aircraft personnel, up to 1548 men.

Other heavy cruisers launched before the war were the *Prinz Eugen, Seydlitz* and *Lützow,* of which only the *Prinz Eugen*

(Germania yards, Kiel, 1938) was completely fitted out at the commencement of hostilities. They displaced 14,240 t (instead of the official 10,000), were 208 m long and, during trials, made 32 knots. Their armament and crew strength was the same as that of the *Blücher*.

Developed from two of the Yorck-Class ships projected during World War I in 1916 but never completed, the battleships *Scharnhorst* (Kriesmarine yards, Wilhelmshaven) and *Gneisenau* (Deutsche Werke, Kiel) were launched in 1936. They displaced 35,400 t and 31,850 t respectively, were 230 m long and made 32 knots. Each carried three triple gun turrets with 28-cm guns. These were projected as twin 38-cm gun turrets but the bigger guns were never fitted because of the war. In addition

they mounted twelve 15-cm, fourteen 10.5-cm, sixteen 3.7-cm, and up to thirty-eight 2-cm anti-aircraft guns, as well as a catapult launcher for four aircraft. They had an ultimate complement of 60 officers and 1780 men.

The German Navy's only aircraft carrier, the *Graf Zeppelin,* was launched from the Germania yards in December 1938 but was never fully completed. She had a displacement of 28,900 t and a length of 262 m. Work had started on a second carrier at the Germania yards in Kiel but, before it was launched, it was broken up in 1940.

The unfinished *Graf Zeppelin* was sunk in Stettin at the end of April 1944, salvaged by the Russians in 1947 and towed to Leningrad. Under way, she was badly damaged by a mine and finally scrapped.

Left: The midship section of the battleship *Gneisenau*. Above her fighting top, the rangefinder for her main armament.
Above: The two after turrets of the heavy cruiser *Prinz Eugen*. A veteran of many bat-tles, she fought at the Battle of the Denmark Strait where the British battle-cruiser *Hood* was sunk in 1941, took part in the break-through of the English Channel in 1943 and, in autumn 1944, fought a rearguard action on the retreat from Memel to Dan-zig, where she picked up refugees and fer-ried them to Copenhagen. In Copenhagen she was taken over by the Americans and in 1947 was sunk in an atom bomb test.

Right: The heavy cruiser *Admiral Hipper* off the Norwegian coast during the war. In April 1940 she took part in the invasion of Norway; in the winter of 1940/41 she attacked merchant shipping in the Atlantic and, during the winter of 1944/45, was sent to the Baltic. On May 3 1945 she was sunk by bombs in Kiel.

Above: A painting by Claus Bergen now at the Mürwik Naval College. It shows the *Bismarck's* last stand against a superior force of British warships in the Atlantic, 300 miles north-west of Quessant.

The *Bismarck* was launched in August 1940 at Blohm & Voss in Hamburg. In May 1941 she sailed with the *Prinz Eugen* via Norway for action against Allied merchant shipping in the Atlantic. On May 24, in the Denmark Strait, she engaged several British heavy warships, among them the *Hood*. After the *Hood* was sunk, the *Bismarck*, only slightly damaged, continued in action. On May 27, having lost her steering and after heavy shell damage from superior British forces, she was scuttled.

The crew of the *Bismarck* renew her camouflage before sailing from Kiel Harbour in March 1941. The bow-wave painted on her side was designed to give the impression of a shorter vessel.

The battleships *Bismarck* and *Tirpitz* were the largest ships of any German navy. Built as replacements for the battleships *Hannover* and *Schleswig-Holstein,* their official displacements were given as 35,000 t. In reality, the *Bismarck* had a displacement of 41,700 t and the *Tirpitz,* 42,900. Both ships were 251 m long and made just on 31 knots. Their heavy armament consisted of two twin gun turrets forward and aft, with a total of eight 38-cm guns, together with twelve 15-cm, sixteen 10.5-cm, sixteen 3.7-cm and, originally, twelve 2-cm anti-aircraft guns. The *Tirpitz* later mounted a further forty-six 2-cm guns. They also carried a double catapult for launching their six aircraft. The *Tirpitz* had a full complement of 108 officers and 2500 men.

Both ships were launched early in the spring of 1939 and were completed during the Second World War.

Left: The battleship *Tirpitz*, the largest ship of any German fleet, lying in Altafjord, Norway, in 1944. She was commissioned in February 1941 at the Kriegsmarine yards in Wilhelmshaven. After several sorties in the Arctic, she was badly damaged by a limpet mine from a British midget submarine in the Altafjord in September 1943 and again, after her repair, by British bombers in April 1944. In November 1944, attacked by special heavy bombs dropped by RAF planes, she capsized near Tromsö and sank with 1204 men.

Left: The destroyer *Z28* (Deschimag, Bremen, 1940), leader of the Destroyer Flotilla. She was lost to British bombers off Sassnitz in March 1945, going down with 150 men.

The first of a new series of twelve torpedo-boats, which included the *Albatros* and *Kondor,* was launched from the Reichsmarine yards at Wilhelmshaven in 1926 (see page 163). This was the 998 t *Möwe* which, with three 10.5-cm cannon and six torpedo tubes, resembled in many details the last torpedo-boats of World War I. Later, with the Type-T 1, the first of which was launched from Schichau in Elbing in 1938, a total of 21 further boats were completed by 1942. These were of 962 t displacement. After them, from 1941 onwards, came the so-called "fleet torpedo-boats" of 1512 t displacement, of which fifteen were put into service by 1944.

The first modern destroyers, starting with the *Z1* (the *Leberecht Maass*), were built at various yards between 1934 and 1938. These were the *Z1* to *Z16*. As well as their series numbers they bore the names of some of Germany's most illustrious sailors. They were, on average, 120 m long and displaced about 2600 t. They had five 12.7-cm cannon, eight torpedo tubes and strong anti-aircraft equipment. At full speed they could make almost 38 knots. Somewhat larger, at 2800 t, the *Z17* to *Z22* were built between 1936 and 1939. These were followed, between the autumn of 1940 and March 1944, by the 3000-t *Z23* to *Z39,* also the *Z43,* her 12.7-cm guns partly replaced by 15-cm pieces. These destroyers usually carried a complement of around 10 officers and 320 men. During the war they were detailed to a variety of tasks, including mine-laying, convoy escort, attacks on merchant shipping and bombardment of shore positions. Their greatest and most tragic operation was the landing in Narvik during the invasion of Norway. Here, ten destroyers, with their commander Commodore Bonte, fell victim to the guns of a superior force of British warships. During the war, out of a total of 40 German destroyers (not counting rebuilt captured enemy ships), 25 were lost.

Above left: The destroyer *Z5,* the *Paul Jacobi* (Deschimag, Bremen, 1936). She served in Norway, the English Channel and at Spitzbergen and was handed over to France in 1946.

Left: The destroyer *Z21* the *Wilhelm Heidkamp* (Deschimag, 1938) sank on April 11 1940 in the bay of Narvik during a battle with British destroyers.

Right: The torpedo-boats *T22* (left) and *T1.* In the foreground, two high-speed torpedo-boats.

Between 1932 and 1939 something like twenty high-speed torpedo-boats (Schnellboote) were built at the Lürssen yards in Vegesack. By the end of the war, the number had risen to about 250. They were mainly used as coastal patrol craft in the Channel, harrying enemy merchant shipping. They were of between 80 and 120 t and were armed with two torpedo tubes and later with light anti-aircraft guns. Their three diesel engines gave them speeds of up to 40 knots. Somewhat reminiscent of torpedo-boats of World War I design, their carvel-built, planked hulls were similar to those of the minesweeping R-Boat series. The latter, however, had only two engines, made only 20 knots and were mainly used in sheltered waters for mine-clearing and escort duties.

In addition to these were the approximately 800-t minesweepers, the M-Boat series, which from 1937 onwards were built at various yards and saw constant duty throughout the war as minesweepers and convoy escorts. And there were also the hundreds of converted freighters and fishing craft which, as auxiliary minesweepers, mine barrier breakers, auxiliary cruisers, picket craft and submarine chasers, served their country, unrecognised.

Right: The minesweeper *R23* (Abeking & Rasmussen, Lemwerder, 1936). After the war, she was handed over to the USA.

With the outbreak of the Second World War on September 1 1939, the German Navy was only minimally prepared. In this it differed markedly from its opponents, especially Britain.

Germany had at this time two battleships, three pocket battleships, two heavy and six light cruisers, 20 destroyers, 10 torpedo-boats, 20 high-speed torpedo-boats and 57 submarines. Ill-prepared though it may have been, the Navy had no choice but to go into battle. At first, during the invasion of Norway and the early part of the submarine war, luck seemed to be with them. But, as the first, victorious phase of Germany's conquests on land ran out, the inadequacy of the Navy became only too clear. In January 1943, Dönitz, whom Hitler had appointed as Admiral of the Fleet, relieved his former commander-in-chief, Raeder. The Navy continued to concentrate on the increasingly costly U-boat campaign. Also, hundreds of small vessels, in spite of heavy losses, maintained escort cover for the all-important supply transports along the European coasts and, later, for the withdrawal of troops and refugees from the hard-pressed eastern front. For large-scale, victorious sea battles there was neither the strength nor the opportunity.

Allied losses due to naval actions totalled more than 21 million gross registered tons, of which 70% resulted from submarine strikes. But these were more than made up by the 39 million GRT built during the war.

By the end of the war, the only larger ships in seaworthy condition left to Germany were the *Prinz Eugen*, the *Nürnberg* and a mere thirty destroyers and torpedo-boats. All had to be handed over to the victors.

And so a chapter of German naval history closes. When the final reckoning was made, nearly a hundred years of heroism, sacrifice and loss proved futile. In all the wars they fought—1848/1849, 1864, 1866, 1870/1871, 1914/1918 and 1939/1945— their opponents emerged victorious. In the first four, luck was still with them; in the next to last, their losses at sea were relatively slight; in the last, they were brought to their knees.

Index of Ships' Names

The index covers the names of all German warships mentioned in the text. Launching dates are given in brackets, followed by page references.

Bibliography

Bekker, Cajus: Kampf und Untergang der Kriegsmarine, Hannover 1953

Bekker, Cajus: Die versunkene Flotte, Oldenburg und Hamburg 1964

Bekker, Cajus: Verdammte See, Oldenburg und Hamburg 1971

Bekker, Cajus: Das große Bilderbuch der deutschen Kriegsmarine, Oldenburg und Hamburg 1972

Bessell, Georg: Geschichte Bremerhavens, Bremerhaven 1927

Bessell, Georg: Norddeutscher Lloyd 1857–1957, Bremen o. J.

Gröner, Erich: Die deutschen Kriegsschiffe 1815–1945 — Band I München 1966

Gröner, Erich: Die deutschen Kriegsschiffe 1815–1945 — Band 2 München 1968

Hansen, Heinrich Egon: Beiträge zur Geschichte der deutschen Flotte 1848–1853, Typoskript, Oldenburg 1961

Herzog, Bodo: Die deutsche Kriegsmarine im Kampf 1939–1945, Dorheim 1969

Hubatsch, Walther: Der Admiralstab und die obersten Marinebehörden in Deutschland 1848–1945, Frankfurt/Main 1958

Jane's Fighting Ships, London 1897 ff.

Kronenfels, J. F. v.: Das schwimmende Flottenmaterial der Seemächte, Wien 1881

Le Fleming, H. M.: Warships of World War I, London 1961

Mantey, Eberhard v.: Unsere Marine im Weltkrieg 1914–1918, Berlin 1928

Mantey, Eberhard v.: Marine-Geschichtsfibel, Berlin 1943

Neudeck, Georg und Schröder, Heinr.: Das kleine Buch von der Marine, Kiel und Leipzig 1899

Richter, J. W. Otto: Unsere Marine im deutsch-französischen Kriege, Altenburg 1907

Rickmers 1834–1959, Bremerhaven 1960

Röhr, Albert: Handbuch der deutschen Marinegeschichte Oldenburg und Hamburg 1963

Rohwer, Jürgen: U-Boote, Oldenburg und Hamburg 1962

Rohwer, Jürgen und Hümmelchen, G.: Chronik des Seekrieges 1939–1945, Oldenburg und Hamburg 1968

Ruge, Friedrich: Scapa Flow 1919, Oldenburg und Hamburg 1969

Schmalenbach, Paul: Kurze Geschichte der k. u. k. Marine, Herford 1970

Sokol, A. E.: Seemacht Österreich, Wien-München-Zürich 1972

Taylor, John C.: German Warships — London 1969

Thomer, Egbert: Torpedoboote und Zerstörer, Oldenburg und Hamburg 1964

Weyers Taschenbuch der Kriegsflotten, später Weyers Flottentaschenbuch, München 1900 ff.

Acknowledgments

The author and publisher are indebted to the following institutions and individuals for their kind permission to reproduce the photographs and illustrations which appear in this book: Bayerische Staatsbibliothek, München; Deutsches Schiffahrtsmuseum, Bremerhaven; Foto-Drüppel, Wilhelmshaven; Fockemuseum, Bremen; Heimatmuseum, Bremen-Vegesack; Historische Sammlung der Marineschule Mürwik, Flensburg; Howaldtswerke-Deutsche Werft AG, Kiel; Imperial War Museum, London; Frau Dr. Jobst, Bremen; Kieler Yacht Club, Kiel; Photo Lassen, Flensburg; Walter Lüden, Wyk auf Föhr; Evelinde Manon, Gräfelfing vor München; National Maritime Museum Greenwich, London; Photo Renard, Kiel; Karl F. Schellmann, Kiel; Schiffahrtsmuseum der Oldenburgischen Weserhäfen, Brake; Schleswig-Holsteinische Landesbibliothek, Kiel; Stadtarchiv, Bremerhaven; Gerhard Stalling Verlag (Archiv), Oldenburg; Ferdinand Urbahns, Eutin.